A Gift for

W9-DIH-872

Presented by

Liar! Liar!
Pants on
Fire!

Liar! Liar! Pants on Fire!

Can You Spot the Truth from the Lies?

Jan Payne

Reader's
Digest

The Reader's Digest Association, Inc.
New York, NY/Montreal

A READER'S DIGEST BOOK

Copyright © 2012 Michael O'Mara Books Limited
All rights reserved. Unauthorized reproduction, in any manner, is prohibited.
Reader's Digest is a registered trademark of The Reader's Digest Association, Inc.

First published in Great Britain by Michael O'Mara Books Limited, 9 Lion Yard, Tremadoc Road, London SW47NQ.

FOR READER'S DIGEST
U.S. Editor: Barbara Booth
Consulting Editor: Susan Randol
Proofreader: Meg Ceccolini
Designer: Nick Anderson
Illustrator: Paul Moran
Managing Editor: Lorraine Burton
Senior Art Director: George McKeon
Associate Publisher, Trade Publishing: Rosanne McManus
President and Publisher, Trade Publishing: Harold Clarke
Editor-in-Chief, Reader's Digest North America: Liz Vaccariello
President, Reader's Digest North America: Dan Lagani
President and CEO, Reader's Digest Association, Inc.: Robert H. Guth

Library of Congress Cataloging in Publication Data

Payne, Jan.
  Liar! Liar! Pants on fire! : can you spot the truth among the lies? / Jan Payne ; illustrated by Paul Moran.
     p. cm.
  Includes index.
  "First published in Great Britain by Michael O'Mara Books."
  ISBN 978-1-60652-476-3 (alk. paper) -- ISBN 978-1-60652-478-7
  (epub) -- ISBN 978-1-60652-477-0 (adobe)
  1. Children's questions and answers. I. Moran, Paul, ill. II. Title.
  AG195.P39 2012
  031.02--dc23

                              2012001313

We are committed to both the quality of our products and the service we provide to our customers. We value your comments, so please feel free to contact us.

       The Reader's Digest Association, Inc.
       Adult Trade Publishing
       44 South Broadway
       White Plains, NY 10601

For more Reader's Digest products and information, visit our website:

       www.rd.com (in the United States)
       www.readersdigest.ca (in Canada)

Printed in the United States of America

1 3 5 7 9 10 8 6 4 2

Contents

THE NATURAL WORLD 11

OUR POWERFUL PLANET 47

THE SCIENCE PART 77

SUPER HUMANS 107

Introduction:
True or False?

Did you know butterflies taste with their feet and that jellyfish live forever? That boa constrictors swallow large pigs whole? Or do they? This book is full of fascinating facts and fat fibs—and it's up to you to decipher which is which.

From facts about astonishing animals to incredible inventions and dramatic discoveries, you will have a great time testing your knowledge, while learning some astonishing truths and uncovering some large lies along the way. Then check out the shocking facts that follow to see if your lie-detecting skills are up to snuff.

IT'S UP TO YOU

Here's how it works. Each section contains a list of facts. Check either True or False to indicate your answer. Then turn the page to see if you're right.

THE FACTS	TRUE	FALSE
1. I am an amazing lie detector.	☑	○

There's a chart on pages 138–139 in which you can write down your score for each section. Then find out your grand total by adding up how many of these 200 facts you got right!

So what are you waiting for? Grab a pen and see if you can spot the twisted truths. Why not test your family and friends to see if they know the facts? You never know! You may surprise them with some of the stranger-than-fiction truths waiting to amaze you on these fun-packed pages.

THE NATURAL WORLD

Bizarre Beasties

Why do animals do the things they do? Test your amazing animal expertise to see if you can tell the truths from the lies. Check either the True or False circle beside each question, then turn to pages 14–16 for the truth.

THE FACTS	TRUE	FALSE
1. Koalas never drink.	○	○
2. Pill bugs drink through their bottoms.	○	○
3. A fish called a pancake batfish can fly.	○	○
4. An ant never sleeps.	○	○
5. Dolphins can put one half of their brains to sleep.	○	○
6. Butterflies taste with their feet.	○	○
7. Ermines like to sing to their prey.	○	○

If you think some of these sound fishy, turn the page.

1. KOALAS NEVER DRINK.

FALSE

Koala is an ancient native-Australian word meaning "no drink." In fact, koalas do occasionally take a sip of water, but they get most of their water from the leaves they eat. The leaves of the eucalyptus tree are their leafy snack of choice.

2. PILL BUGS DRINK THROUGH THEIR BOTTOMS.

TRUE

Pill bugs take in some water with their food, but when they are really thirsty, they drink through their bottoms. To vacuum up the water, they use things called uropods, which are little tubes positioned under their tails. The uropods suck up water when pressed together and held against moist surfaces.

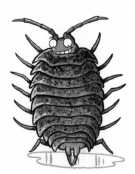

3. A FISH CALLED A PANCAKE BATFISH CAN FLY.

FALSE

The pancake batfish, a fish that lives in the deep waters of the Gulf of Mexico, can't fly. It can, however, "walk" on its fins. It has stubby fins, which it moves like legs, enabling it to hop around. Some people say the batfish looks like a pancake with feet.

4. AN ANT NEVER SLEEPS.

FALSE

Actually, ants do sleep, but the ants in a colony are never all asleep at the same time. They take turns so there are always some awake to protect the nest. Ants take hundreds of short naps—as many as 250 a day—for about one minute at a time. The queen ant, on the other hand, gets luxury royal treatment and sleeps for up to nine hours a day.

5. DOLPHINS CAN PUT ONE HALF OF THEIR BRAINS TO SLEEP.

TRUE

Dolphins have to remain alert for days at a time to protect themselves from predators. To do this, they use a clever trick to stop themselves from getting tired. They put one half of their brains to sleep for a number of hours. When that half is rested, they wake it up and switch off the other half.

6. BUTTERFLIES TASTE WITH THEIR FEET.

TRUE

Butterflies have taste sensors on their feet, so they can tell if something is good to eat simply by standing on it. In fact, they don't even have mouths; once they find some nectar, they use a long tube named a proboscis to suck it out of flowers. *Slurp!*

7. ERMINES LIKE TO SING TO THEIR PREY.

FALSE

Ermines, which are related to weasels, are better dancers than they are singers. They hunt all kinds of animals, but they like nothing better than a tasty rabbit. When an ermine spots a rabbit, it does a kind of bizarre break-dance routine, with lots of leaps and twists, in order to get close to it. The rabbit becomes hypnotized by the ermine's crazy moves and stays rooted to the spot while the hunter boogies closer and closer, until it's finally close enough to make a grab for its startled victim.

Terrible Teeth

The animal world is full of marvelous molars and fearsome fangs, but are the facts about some of nature's nastiest gnashers true or false? Mark the boxes, then check pages 18–20 for the toothy truth.

THE FACTS	TRUE	FALSE
1. A walrus can walk on its teeth.	O	O
2. Sharks don't use their teeth for chewing.	O	O
3. Alligators will often give you a toothy grin.	O	O
4. A spider chews its food before it swallows it.	O	O
5. A snail has more than 25,000 teeth.	O	O
6. The male angler fish uses his teeth to find the love of his life and never lets her go.	O	O
7. The blue whale has the largest teeth in the animal world.	O	O

Turn the page to find out the "tooth!"

1. A WALRUS CAN WALK ON ITS TEETH.

TRUE

Walruses use their two huge tusks, which are nearly 3 feet (1 m) long, to pull themselves out of the water. They can also use their teeth to help them "walk" across the ground. The walrus's scientific name *(Odobenus rosmarus)* means "tooth-walking sea horse," which is quite a mouthful!

2. SHARKS DON'T USE THEIR TEETH FOR CHEWING.

TRUE

While sharks can have up to 3,000 chompers in their mouths at a time, they really only use them to snatch and tear their food apart before gulping down the chunks.

3. ALLIGATORS WILL OFTEN GIVE YOU A TOOTHY GRIN.

TRUE

Though an alligator's teeth are hidden when its mouth is closed, it often sits around with its mouth open in a "grin." You don't want to be around when an alligator is showing off its pearly whites. The force of its bite is about the same as getting crushed by a falling car!

4. A SPIDER CHEWS ITS FOOD BEFORE IT SWALLOWS IT.

FALSE

A spider doesn't chew its food. When a spider finds an insect caught in its sticky web, it wraps the insect up in silk and uses its fangs to inject poison. When it is time to eat, the spider smears its victim with strong digestive juices and waits patiently for the snack to dissolve. When the insect has turned to mush, the spider sucks it up like bug soup. Yummy!

5. A SNAIL HAS MORE THAN 25,000 TEETH.

TRUE

A snail's ribbonlike tongue is lined with microscopic munchers that look like the spikes on the edge of a saw blade. The snail uses its tiny teeth to slice off morsels of food before digesting them.

6. THE MALE ANGLER FISH USES HIS TEETH TO FIND THE LOVE OF HIS LIFE AND NEVER LETS HER GO.

TRUE

When a male angler fish finds a female, he hangs on to her with his small, hooklike teeth and doesn't let her go. He releases a substance that digests the skin of her body and the skin of his mouth so they stick together. Over time the male gradually wastes away, losing his brain, internal organs, and even his eyes. And you thought getting your braces stuck mid-smooch was bad!

7. THE BLUE WHALE HAS THE LARGEST TEETH IN THE ANIMAL WORLD.

FALSE

The blue whale is the largest animal on Earth, but it doesn't have any teeth. Instead, its mouth is filled with plates, called baleen, which are covered in bristles. The whale traps its food—tiny, shrimplike animals called krill—in the bristles and then gulps them down.

Eat or Be Eaten

Some creatures have terrible taste when it comes to food. Are these vomit-worthy facts hard or easy to swallow? Mark your answers, then check pages 22–24 to reveal all.

THE FACTS	TRUE	FALSE
1. Koala babies eat their mother's poop.	◯	◯
2. The housefly throws up its food, then eats it again.	◯	◯
3. The red snapper fish has a sea louse for a tongue.	◯	◯
4. The Venus flytrap plant spits out things it doesn't like.	◯	◯
5. Rabbits eat their own poop.	◯	◯
6. The starfish's stomach is outside its body.	◯	◯
7. Cows don't fart after eating.	◯	◯

Find out the farty facts by turning the page.

1. KOALA BABIES EAT THEIR MOTHER'S POOP.

TRUE

When a baby koala is ready to move on from its mother's milk, it needs to get used to a diet of eucalyptus leaves. These leaves contain poisons that would make a young koala very sick, so the mother koala produces a special poop with some of the poisons taken out, and the baby eats it.

2. THE HOUSEFLY THROWS UP ITS FOOD, THEN EATS IT AGAIN.

TRUE

A housefly can only eat liquid food. It spits digestive juices on the food to help dissolve it and then sucks it up. If the food hasn't dissolved fully, the fly regurgitates, or throws it up, and eats it again.

3. THE RED SNAPPER FISH HAS A SEA LOUSE FOR A TONGUE.

TRUE

A parasite is a creature that lives in or on another animal. Red snapper fish often have a parasite living in their mouths. This cringe-worthy creature sucks blood from the fish's tongue until the tongue withers and dies. Then the parasite takes the place of the tongue so that the fish can continue to eat. Every time the fish eats, the parasite keeps a little bit of the food for itself. Sneaky!

4. THE VENUS FLYTRAP PLANT SPITS OUT THINGS IT DOESN'T LIKE.

FALSE

The Venus flytrap has special pairs of leaves that are covered in tiny hairs and have spiny teeth along their edges. When a fly or insect touches the hairs, the two halves close, trapping the prey. However, there's a small gap around the edges, so if the prey is too tiny to bother with, it's allowed to escape.

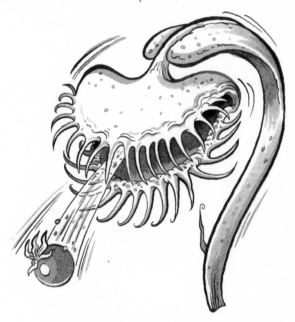

5. RABBITS EAT THEIR OWN POOP.

TRUE

Rabbits actually need to eat some of the stuff they poop out, called cecotropes. These poopy pellets have loads of good vitamins and help rabbits digest food. Tasty!

6. THE STARFISH'S STOMACH IS OUTSIDE ITS BODY.

FALSE

The starfish doesn't have a stomach on the outside of its body, but it can turn itself inside out when it wants to eat something that's too big to fit in its mouth. So the starfish pushes its stomach out through its mouth to digest the food. When it's done, the starfish puts its tummy away again.

7. COWS DON'T FART AFTER EATING.

FALSE

A cow can eat up to 90 pounds (41 kg) of food a day, which gives it loads of gas. Cows are constantly burping and farting, releasing more than 79 gallons (300 L) of smelly methane gas every day. And with more than a billion cows on the planet, that's a lot of gas!

24

Serious Survival Skills

The natural world is filled with tough reptiles, indestructible insects, and other amazingly adaptable organisms. But are these facts about the strongest survivors true or false? Mark the boxes below, then check pages 26–28 to see if you're right.

THE FACTS	TRUE	FALSE
1. The Spanish ribbed newt is known as Robin Hood because it protects itself with bows and arrows.	○	○
2. Crocodiles are such great survivors, they even lived when dinosaurs roamed the Earth.	○	○
3. Lizards shed their tails to escape predators.	○	○
4. Cockroaches can survive without their heads.	○	○
5. No plant is tough enough to survive in Antarctica.	○	○
6. Sharks are so adaptable, they have even swum in space.	○	○
7. An opossum is a furry faker that plays dead to escape predators.	○	○

1. THE SPANISH RIBBED NEWT IS KNOWN AS ROBIN HOOD BECAUSE IT PROTECTS ITSELF WITH BOWS AND ARROWS.

FALSE

The Spanish ribbed newt doesn't use a set of bows and arrows, but this tough little fighter goes to extreme lengths to protect itself. When an enemy comes near, the ribbed newt pushes its ribs through its skin to make a row of sharp, pointed arrows. Each "arrow" is tipped with poison from the newt's skin to keep predators away.

2. CROCODILES ARE SUCH GREAT SURVIVORS, THEY EVEN LIVED WHEN DINOSAURS ROAMED THE EARTH.

TRUE

Crocodiles have been on the planet for over 200 million years. They existed alongside dinosaurs—but while dinosaurs became extinct 65 million years ago, crocodiles survived. These cunning creatures have keen senses, are amazing hunters, and can go without food for long periods of time, making them one of Earth's super-survivors.

3. LIZARDS SHED THEIR TAILS TO ESCAPE PREDATORS.

TRUE

If a predator grabs a lizard by its tail, very often the tail is all it will get to eat. The lizard is able to shed its tail, leaving it wriggling about in the surprised predator's mouth. The lizard itself escapes to live another day . . . and, eventually, grow a new tail.

4. COCKROACHES CAN SURVIVE WITHOUT THEIR HEADS.

TRUE

Since they can survive for many days without food and water, cockroaches don't need their heads to keep going. Unlike humans, cockroaches don't have a nose on their head. Instead, they breathe through parts of their body. A cockroach's body seals over a cut quickly, so a cockroach won't bleed to death when it loses its head. It can survive for several weeks without one. Even grosser, the head can live on for hours even without the body. Talk about a brawny bug!

5. NO PLANT IS TOUGH ENOUGH TO SURVIVE IN ANTARCTICA.

FALSE

Antarctica is a frozen desert, and only the most stubborn creatures can survive there. However, quite a few kinds of simple plants, such as mosses and tiny plantlike organisms called algae, do live in some parts of the Antarctic. Lichens, which are half algae and half fungus, are even tougher. They have been found close to the South Pole, coping with the longest, darkest, coldest winter in the world.

6. SHARKS ARE SO ADAPTABLE, THEY HAVE EVEN SWUM IN SPACE.

FALSE

Sharks haven't made it to space, but an amazingly adaptable fish called the mummichog became the first fish in space. It swam in zero gravity on a mission in 1973. It is probably the world's toughest fish, since it is also able to live in fresh- or saltwater—something most of its finned friends can't do—and can survive in badly polluted waters. That's one strong swimmer.

7. AN OPOSSUM IS A FURRY FAKER THAT PLAYS DEAD TO ESCAPE PREDATORS.

TRUE

These furry fighters are fine actors. When they feel threatened, they pretend to be dead with Hollywood-worthy acting skills,

known as "playing possum." An opossum lies on the ground with its tongue hanging out of its mouth and releases a stinky smell to keep animals from checking it out. Most animals don't like to scavenge, which means they don't like to eat meat that is already dead when they find it. So playing dead keeps opossums safe from predators.

Superpowers

Some of the world's cleverest creatures have amazing abilities, but can you tell the real superpowers from the fakes? Mark your answers below, then check pages 30–32 for the right stuff.

THE FACTS	TRUE	FALSE
1. The short-horned lizard spits blood to frighten its enemies.	○	○
2. A bloodhound's sense of smell is thousands of times stronger than a human's.	○	○
3. The torpedo fish electrocutes its prey.	○	○
4. Geckos have super climbing powers that allow them to scale slippery surfaces, such as glass.	○	○
5. Jellyfish can live forever.	○	○
6. A snakebite can kill an elephant but not a honey badger.	○	○
7. The hairworm can control a cricket's mind.	○	○

Look into my eyes and tell me the truth.

1. THE SHORT-HORNED LIZARD SPITS BLOOD TO FRIGHTEN ITS ENEMIES.

FALSE

It's actually weirder than that. A short-horned lizard squirts blood from its **eyes** when it is attacked and can shoot the disgusting-tasting liquid up to 10 feet (3 m). It can also inflate its body so that it looks like a spiny balloon.

2. A BLOODHOUND'S SENSE OF SMELL IS THOUSANDS OF TIMES STRONGER THAN A HUMAN'S.

TRUE

These superdogs have such a keen sense of smell that they are often seen as heroes. They have 4 billion smell-detecting cells in their noses, and the wrinkles around their faces help guide any stray smell particles into their big nostrils. Bloodhounds are used by the police, because their sensitive snouts can help track down missing people and sniff out criminals.

3. THE TORPEDO FISH ELECTROCUTES ITS PREY.

TRUE

The torpedo fish, also known as the electric ray, can produce up to 200 volts of electricity, which is enough power to kill its prey immediately. Supplying the shock is a pair of organs located in each of the fins behind this fierce fish's eyes.

4. GECKOS HAVE SUPER CLIMBING POWERS THAT ALLOW THEM TO SCALE SLIPPERY SURFACES, SUCH AS GLASS.

TRUE

These clever climbers have millions of microscopic hairs on the bottom of their feet. The hairs act like a super-sticky glue and allow geckos to cling to almost any kind of surface. The hairs aren't actually covered in any kind of sticky substance, so the geckos don't get stuck, and they don't leave a messy trail as they climb, either.

5. JELLYFISH CAN LIVE FOREVER.

TRUE

A certain kind of jellyfish can live forever. . . . Well, sort of. Scientists say that these tiny jellyfish can age backward. That is, once they are fully grown, some of the jellyfish transform back into a polyp, which is the form of a baby jellyfish. They can then grow into adults again. This jellyfish is the only animal capable of this, and it can repeat this cycle over and over. So it's almost as though they can live forever!

6. A SNAKEBITE CAN KILL AN ELEPHANT BUT NOT A HONEY BADGER.

TRUE

The honey badger is one of the fiercest animals in the world. This fearless hunter will steal prey from venomous snakes and even tackle the snakes themselves. A bite from a puff adder—Africa's most dangerous snake—contains enough venom to kill five humans, but for a honey badger it just stings a bit for a few hours.

7. THE HAIRWORM CAN CONTROL A CRICKET'S MIND.

TRUE

This powerful parasite makes its home inside a cricket, where it produces a cocktail of chemicals that affects the way the cricket thinks and behaves. Eventually, the hairworm convinces the cricket to plunge into water. Sadly, the cricket drowns. The hairworm, however, emerges from the dead cricket and looks for a mate in the water.

Peculiar Parenting

There are loads of miserable mothers, dastardly dads, and some perfect parents in the natural world, but can you tell which are the facts and which are lies? Decide whether the facts are true or false, and mark the boxes below. Check pages 34–36 to see if you're right.

THE FACTS	TRUE	FALSE
1. The female emperor penguin lays her egg on the ice and leaves it all alone there until it hatches.	O	O
2. The Siamese fighting fish protects its young by blowing bubbles.	O	O
3. A bird called the hooded grebe lays one egg at a time so she can love and spoil just one chick.	O	O
4. Female grizzly bears kill their cubs.	O	O
5. Elephant seals would rather adopt than look after their own babies.	O	O
6. Black eagle mothers let their kids fight bloody battles.	O	O
7. The Nile crocodile eats its young while they are still in their eggs.	O	O
8. Male sea horses can bear as many as 600 baby sea horses.	O	O

1. THE FEMALE EMPEROR PENGUIN LAYS HER EGG ON THE ICE AND LEAVES IT ALL ALONE THERE UNTIL IT HATCHES.

FALSE

After the mother penguin lays an egg, she goes off to find food. But the father puts the egg on top of his feet and pulls a flap of skin over it to keep it warm. Then the dad stands in the harsh winter and waits for it to hatch. If the egg falls on to the freezing ice, the baby penguin will die.

2. THE SIAMESE FIGHTING FISH PROTECTS ITS YOUNG BY BLOWING BUBBLES.

TRUE

The male Siamese fighting fish is an amazing dad. He makes a nest of bubbles to protect the eggs laid by his mate. He watches over the eggs and constantly repairs the nest by spitting more bubbles. If an egg falls out of the bubble nest, he carefully puts it back. However, the baby fish need to swim away soon after hatching, because the kind dad may try to eat them!

3. A BIRD CALLED THE HOODED GREBE LAYS ONE EGG AT A TIME SO SHE CAN LOVE AND SPOIL JUST ONE CHICK.

FALSE

Birds called hooded grebes lay two eggs at a time, and both parents keep them warm until hatching time. The egg that hatches first becomes mama's cherished chick. In fact, both parents abandon the other egg as soon as the first egg hatches, leaving baby number two to fend for itself.

4. FEMALE GRIZZLY BEARS KILL THEIR CUBS.

FALSE

The female grizzly bear is one of the most protective mothers on the planet. She will go to great lengths to keep her cubs safe. Male grizzly bears often kill the cubs of other males, so to keep them safe, moms take their cubs to remote areas where there aren't many other bears around.

5. ELEPHANT SEALS WOULD RATHER ADOPT THAN LOOK AFTER THEIR OWN BABIES.

FALSE

The northern elephant seal is a great mother. She takes care of her own baby, or pup, often going without food just to stay close. But if she loses her pup, she will go to any length to get another. She'll adopt orphan pups or even steal one from another mother!

6. BLACK EAGLE MOTHERS LET THEIR KIDS FIGHT BLOODY BATTLES.

TRUE

When baby black eagles fight, the naughty kids don't get a time-out. Their mom lets them fight violently—to the death. Two eggs are laid, but the parents can only catch enough prey to bring up one chick. They let the two fight it out so that the stronger baby— almost always the older one—survives.

7. THE NILE CROCODILE EATS ITS YOUNG WHILE THEY ARE STILL IN THEIR EGGS.

FALSE

A mother crocodile watches over her eggs, waiting for the moment when the tiny crocs make chirruping sounds inside. Then she takes an egg gently in her mouth and rolls it around to help it hatch. After the eggs have hatched, she continues to look after her babies until they are old enough to feed themselves.

8. MALE SEA HORSES CAN BEAR AS MANY AS 600 BABY SEA HORSES.

TRUE

In the world of sea horses, the role of baby bearing is carried out by the male, who can have anywhere from 200 to 600 babies at one time! To impress a potential mate and show off his birthing pouch, a male sea horse will fill up his pouch with as much water as he can to indicate his strength and ability to carry a load of baby sea horses through three weeks of pregnancy and 72 hours of labor. After the babies are born, the female assumes the role of finding food for them. Within just a few weeks the male sea horse will fill up its pouch once more to let the female know he is ready to do it all over again.

Delightful Dinos

Dinosaurs ruled the Earth for 185 million years, but how long will it take you to spot the mistruths about these amazing animals? Mark your answers below, then check pages 38–40 to see if you're a dino expert.

THE FACTS	**TRUE**	**FALSE**
1. The T-Rex was the fastest dinosaur.	○	○
2. The name "dinosaur" comes from the verb "to dine" or "to eat," because dinosaurs ate constantly.	○	○
3. The smallest dinosaurs were no bigger than chickens.	○	○
4. The Nigersaurus was used as a vacuum cleaner by other dinosaurs.	○	○
5. Dinosaurs died out because the big ones ate all the little ones and then starved to death because they had nothing left to eat.	○	○
6. The Pterodactyl was a flying reptile.	○	○
7. Dinosaurs grew so large because the prey they ate was huge, too.	○	○

1. THE T-REX WAS THE FASTEST DINOSAUR.

FALSE

The T-Rex could run at speeds of only 15 miles (24 km) per hour, less than half as fast as the Gallimimus, a fast-moving birdlike dinosaur that could move at speeds of up to 35 miles (56 km) per hour.

2. THE NAME "DINOSAUR" COMES FROM THE VERB "TO DINE" OR "TO EAT," BECAUSE DINOSAURS ATE CONSTANTLY.

FALSE

The name "dinosaur" comes from two Greek words that mean "terrible lizard." In fact, dinosaurs were not lizards, and only a few were terrible. Most dinosaurs were about as fierce as cows and spent their time munching on leafy greens.

3. THE SMALLEST DINOSAURS WERE NO BIGGER THAN CHICKENS.

TRUE

The smallest dinosaur was the Compsognathus, which was the same size as a chicken. It walked on two long, thin legs and had two short arms with clawed fingers on each hand. It could run fast and ate insects and lizards.

4. THE NIGERSAURUS WAS USED AS A VACUUM CLEANER BY OTHER DINOSAURS.

FALSE

The Nigersaurus did have a mouth that looked and worked exactly like a vacuum cleaner, but it didn't do any cleaning. This delightful dinosaur had wide lips and over 500 tiny teeth that it used to chomp really close to the ground and suck up grass and ferns. When it wore down its teeth with the constant chomping, other teeth, which were stashed in rows behind the front teeth, took over. The Nigersaurus had a very long neck, so it could mow down loads of plants while standing in one spot.

5. DINOSAURS DIED OUT BECAUSE THE BIG ONES ATE ALL THE LITTLE ONES AND THEN STARVED TO DEATH BECAUSE THEY HAD NOTHING LEFT TO EAT.

FALSE

Scientists have many ideas about why dinosaurs died out, or became extinct, but this isn't one of them. The most popular idea is that a giant meteorite hit the Earth, throwing up a huge dust cloud. This would have quickly changed the entire world's climate for a long time, perhaps killing the dinosaurs. Of course, no one knows what happened for sure, but scientists are learning more all the time.

6. THE PTERODACTYL WAS A FLYING REPTILE.

TRUE

These high-flyers were winged reptiles, related to dinosaurs. Their arms were modified into wings, with a leathery web connecting the tip of the fourth finger—which was 10 times longer than the other fingers—to the foot.

7. DINOSAURS GREW SO LARGE BECAUSE THE PREY THEY ATE WAS HUGE, TOO.

FALSE

Many of the largest dinosaurs, such as the Brontosaurus, which grew up to 90 feet (27 m) long, were actually plant eaters. They were so huge because the plants they ate were really tough to digest. The dinos' teeth weren't very good at chewing, so their stomachs had to break down the food instead. To do this, they needed to be huge, rumbling digestion tanks—and big stomachs needed to be carried in big bodies!

Horrible Habits

If you think your friend's nose-picking habit is disgusting, wait until you see what some of these animals are up to. Decide which are the true facts. Then turn to pages 42–45 to find out the truth.

THE FACTS	TRUE	FALSE
1. Bush babies drink their own pee.	O	O
2. Hagfish cover themselves in mucus.	O	O
3. The boa constrictor swallows large pigs—whole!	O	O
4. Vampire bats drink blood only from dead animals.	O	O
5. Camels spit at people or animals that threaten them.	O	O
6. Cats swallow their own hair and cough up furry balls of it.	O	O
7. Dogs sniff each other's bottoms.	O	O

Can you sniff out a lie?

1. BUSH BABIES DRINK THEIR OWN PEE.

FALSE

Bush babies are small, fluffy animals related to monkeys. They look far too cute to have a horrible habit, but one very unpleasant thing they do is catch their pee in their hands. When a bush baby climbs and jumps through the trees, every time it grabs a branch, it leaves a smelly handprint of pee behind, which tells other bush babies where it has been. Pee is very important in bush babies' love lives, too—a male bush baby lets a female know that he likes her by peeing on her. Charming!

2. HAGFISH COVER THEMSELVES IN MUCUS.

TRUE

The hagfish has been named the most disgusting sea creature in the world, because it covers itself with huge amounts of sticky mucus to escape predators. It also rubs slime on its prey to stop it from breathing. Mmm! Booger-covered snack, anyone? When the hagfish has more mucus over its body than even it can bear and wants to get rid of some of the goo, it ties its long, thin body in a knot, then passes the knot down its length to scrape off the gloopy gunk.

3. THE BOA CONSTRICTOR SWALLOWS LARGE PIGS—WHOLE!

TRUE

This scary snake has terrible table manners and never chews its food before swallowing—not even if it's a pig or a deer. The boa constrictor overpowers its prey by squeezing the life out of it. Then it opens its mouth to an enormous size and crams the animal in whole. This leaves the boa with a huge bulge in its belly, so it slithers slowly and carefully away to a quiet spot, where it spends a week or longer lying around, gradually digesting its monster meal.

4. VAMPIRE BATS DRINK BLOOD ONLY FROM DEAD ANIMALS.

FALSE

Vampire bats prefer warm blood from living animals or humans. They wait until their victim is asleep, and then they search for a part of the body that isn't covered with hair so they can get a good bite. When they have made a hole in the skin with their fangs, the bats scarf down the blood like a warm glass of milk. Their saliva contains a chemical called draculin, which stops the blood from clotting as it would normally, so the wound continues to bleed for a long time. If some vampire bats in the colony don't manage to feed in the night, the others will help them out with a meal of vomited-up blood.

5. CAMELS SPIT AT PEOPLE OR ANIMALS THAT THREATEN THEM.

FALSE

When a camel feels threatened, it brings up the contents of its stomach, along with saliva, and spits it at whatever or whoever is bothering it. The vile vomit is meant to distract, pester, or surprise whatever is threatening the camel. While camels will aim a stomach-churning mouthful at people when they are very annoyed, this spiteful spitting is mostly used to settle disputes with other camels over things like whose turn it is to drink at the watering hole.

6. CATS SWALLOW THEIR OWN HAIR AND COUGH UP FURRY BALLS OF IT.

TRUE

Cats are quite enthusiastic about cleaning themselves. When a cat wants to get clean, it licks its fur, but loads of tiny hairs get stuck in the cat's rough tongue, especially if it is a long-haired cat. Those hairs get swallowed and can upset the kitty's tummy. When too much hair is swallowed, the cat pukes up a disgusting lumpy mass of stuck-together hair. If you don't want your cat to suffer from fur balls, give it a good combing from time to time to help get rid of all the loose fur.

7. DOGS SNIFF EACH OTHER'S BOTTOMS.

TRUE

Dogs have an extra gland around their bottoms that gives off a smell. Each dog releases a unique scent, so smelling one another's bottoms is a way of recognizing and meeting other dogs. Scientists say that dogs can learn a lot from sniffing other dogs' bottoms. Occasionally, the glands can get blocked up, which is painful for the dog, and the stinky gunk inside needs to be emptied out by a vet. The vet will probably want to wear nose plugs when carrying out this most revolting of tasks.

OUR
POWERFUL
PLANET

Highest, Hottest, Deepest, Fastest

Find out if you're the smartest by spotting the truths about the highest, deepest, longest, fastest, hottest, coldest, driest things on the planet. Choose which seem to ring true, then turn to pages 50–52 for the answers.

THE FACTS	TRUE	FALSE
1. Everest is the planet's highest mountain.	○	○
2. The amount of water flowing over Victoria Falls every hour would flush 5 million toilets.	○	○
3. The Empire State Building would fill the Earth's deepest trench.	○	○
4. The fastest glacier moves 41,339 feet (12,600 m) every year.	○	○
5. The hottest place on Earth has an average annual temperature of 94°F (35°C).	○	○
6. The coldest temperature on Earth ever recorded was at the North Pole.	○	○
7. The driest place on Earth is the Sahara Desert.	○	○

1. EVEREST IS THE PLANET'S HIGHEST MOUNTAIN.

FALSE

At 29,035 feet (8,850 m), Mount Everest is the highest mountain above sea level, but if you include mountains that are partially underwater, beneath the sea, Hawaii's Mauna Kea is much taller, at 33,480 feet (10,205 m). A mere 13,796 feet (4,205 m) of the mountain is above sea level.

2. THE AMOUNT OF WATER FLOWING OVER VICTORIA FALLS EVERY HOUR WOULD FLUSH 5 MILLION TOILETS.

TRUE

Victoria Falls, which is located on the Zambezi River in Africa, is a staggering 354 feet (108 m) high and 5,604 feet (1,708 m) wide. The falls aren't the highest in the world, but the water that flows over them forms the largest sheet of falling water in the world. The water thundering over the falls would flush 83,692 toilets per second, or 5 million per hour.

3. THE EMPIRE STATE BUILDING WOULD FILL THE EARTH'S DEEPEST TRENCH.

FALSE

The Mariana Trench in the Pacific Ocean is, as far as scientists know, the deepest point on Earth. Within the trench lies Challenger Deep, the bottom of which is an incredible 35,837 feet (10,923 m) below the ocean's surface. It is so deep that it would take almost 29 Empire State Buildings stacked on top of each other to reach the surface.

4. THE FASTEST GLACIER MOVES 41,339 FEET (12,600 M) EVERY YEAR.

TRUE

A glacier is a thick sheet of ice that forms over thousands of years as snow falls and presses together into a huge mass. The sheer size and weight of a glacier makes it flow downhill like a very slow river. In 2003 scientists measured the speed of the world's fastest moving glacier, Jakobshavn Isbræ in Greenland, at 41,339 feet (12,600 m) per year. Where a glacier meets the sea, it often cracks and pieces break off, falling into the sea as icebergs. When glaciers and icebergs melt, the water released makes the sea levels rise. Many scientists believe that global warming is increasing the speeds of glaciers and their melt rates.

5. THE HOTTEST PLACE ON EARTH HAS AN AVERAGE ANNUAL TEMPERATURE OF 94°F (35°C).

TRUE

The Danakil Depression is a desert located in Ethiopia, Africa, and is the hottest place on Earth. It is an area of spectacular volcanic

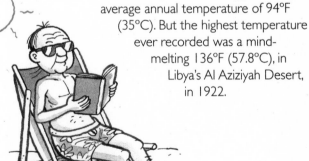

activity, with hot and stinky springs of bubbling sulfur that smell like rotten eggs, and an average annual temperature of 94°F (35°C). But the highest temperature ever recorded was a mind-melting 136°F (57.8°C), in Libya's Al Aziziyah Desert, in 1922.

6. THE COLDEST TEMPERATURE ON EARTH EVER RECORDED WAS AT THE NORTH POLE.

FALSE

The continent of Antarctica is much colder than the North Pole. On July 21, 1983, at a Russian research center called Vostok Station, a record low of −128°F (−89°C) was documented. Winter temperatures in Antarctica tend to be a lot colder because it is much higher above sea level than the North Pole.

7. THE DRIEST PLACE ON EARTH IS THE SAHARA DESERT.

FALSE

The Atacama Desert in South America is the driest place in the world. In some parts, tests have shown that rain hasn't fallen for more than 20 million years. Ironically, in spite of its record-breaking drought, the Atacama lies next to the Pacific Ocean, which is the world's largest body of water.

Danger! Danger!

Our amazing planet is home to some deadly disasters, but are these facts about some of the planet's most extreme events really true? Check pages 54–56 to find out.

THE FACTS	TRUE	FALSE
1. All deadly forest fires are caused by humans.	○	○
2. An earthquake under the ocean can destroy places hundreds of miles away.	○	○
3. Hurricane winds blow fastest at the middle, or eye, of the storm.	○	○
4. An ocean whirlpool, or maelstrom, can pull boats down to the seabed.	○	○
5. Lightning can strike from a clear blue sky, with no thunderstorm overhead.	○	○
6. An avalanche can happen if someone yells on a snow-covered mountain.	○	○
7. When Mount Vesuvius erupted in A.D. 79, a lava flow destroyed Pompeii and Herculaneum.	○	○

1. ALL DEADLY FOREST FIRES ARE CAUSED BY HUMANS.

FALSE

Most forest fires are started accidentally by humans, or even on purpose, but wildfires do happen naturally, too. They can be caused by lightning hitting the Earth, volcanic eruptions, or even by sparks from rocks striking each other during rockfalls. Wildfires are very dangerous. In hot weather, when vegetation is particularly dry, fires can sweep through areas at great speed, destroying everything in their path.

2. AN EARTHQUAKE UNDER THE OCEAN CAN DESTROY PLACES HUNDREDS OF MILES AWAY.

TRUE

An underwater earthquake creates waves that travel for thousands of miles. As they reach land, the waves pile up into a huge wall of water, known as a tsunami. It can destroy everything in its path. In December 2004 a tsunami in the Indian Ocean killed more than 250,000 people in 14 countries.

3. HURRICANE WINDS BLOW FASTEST AT THE MIDDLE, OR EYE, OF THE STORM.

FALSE

A hurricane begins in tropical regions. Warm air rises into a mass of swirling clouds that start to spin, forming a hurricane that can measure up to 310 miles (500 km) wide, with wind speeds of up to 150 miles (240 km) per hour. If the hurricane reaches land, its power can devastate an area. When the middle, or eye, of the storm passes, everything becomes still and quiet, but don't be fooled into thinking it's safe to go outside. It's just a temporary pause before the rest of the storm arrives to wreak havoc.

4. AN OCEAN WHIRLPOOL, OR MAELSTROM, CAN PULL BOATS DOWN TO THE SEABED.

FALSE

A maelstrom is a gigantic whirlpool in the sea that happens when powerful currents of water spin in a circle due to the pull of strong tides. In some whirlpools, water is pulled down toward the seabed in a swirling funnel—like water draining from a bath. In stories and legends, maelstroms sucked boats to the bottom of the sea, but in reality, although the strong currents in a maelstrom could damage a boat, it's unlikely that it would disappear down the center of the whirling waters.

5. LIGHTNING CAN STRIKE FROM A CLEAR BLUE SKY, WITH NO THUNDERSTORM OVERHEAD.

TRUE

Lightning strikes the planet around 50 times a second, usually when there's a thunderstorm overhead. Occasionally, lightning travels from a thunderstorm across clear skies, hitting the ground up to 25 miles (40 km) away. It's known as a "bolt from the blue." You should wait inside for half an hour after a thunderstorm to make sure you won't get hit by a sudden bolt from above.

6. AN AVALANCHE CAN HAPPEN IF SOMEONE YELLS ON A SNOW-COVERED MOUNTAIN.

FALSE

In movies and TV shows, avalanches are triggered when someone shouts or fires a gun. In reality, this isn't powerful enough to start one. Many avalanches are caused when the weight of a person crossing an unstable slope dislodges the snow, causing it to rush down the mountain, often taking the person with it.

7. WHEN MOUNT VESUVIUS ERUPTED IN A.D. 79, A LAVA FLOW DESTROYED POMPEII AND HERCULANEUM.

FALSE

It is true that in A.D. 79 Italy's Mount Vesuvius erupted. The towns of Pompeii and Herculaneum were destroyed, but not by a lava flow. After the eruption a huge cloud of gas and dust rushed down the mountain in what's known as a pyroclastic flow. Until recently, scientists thought that the people in the towns were suffocated by the gases, but they have now shown that the flow had an intense heat of up to 1,112°F (600°C) that killed instantly. The bodies were then covered by volcanic ash, which has preserved the disastrous moment for almost 2,000 years.

Wacky Weather

Our planet is home to some wild weather, but can you tell the fakes from the facts? Read the facts below, record your answers, then reveal the truth by turning to pages 58–60.

THE FACTS	TRUE	FALSE
1. Hailstones can be as big as tennis balls.	○	○
2. The average monthly snowfall at the South Pole is greater than the amount Alaska receives in a year.	○	○
3. In 2008 an upside-down rainbow appeared in the sky over Cambridge, England.	○	○
4. Cows can predict the weather.	○	○
5. In Venezuela a single lightning storm raged for 360 days.	○	○
6. Balls of fire sometimes float through the air during thunderstorms.	○	○
7. It can rain frogs and fish.	○	○
8. During a thunderstorm, street lamps and ships' masts may spark blue flames that can't be extinguished.	○	○

1. HAILSTONES CAN BE AS BIG AS TENNIS BALLS.

TRUE

In fact, hailstones can be bigger than tennis balls. The largest one found to date fell during a storm in South Dakota in 2010, and at 8 inches (20 cm) across, it was similar in size to your head! Hail forms when raindrops are driven high into the atmosphere by air currents, where they freeze. Then the heavy balls of ice fall as hailstones.

2. THE AVERAGE MONTHLY SNOWFALL AT THE SOUTH POLE IS GREATER THAN THE AMOUNT ALASKA RECEIVES IN A YEAR.

FALSE

Strange as it may seem, snow hardly ever falls at the South Pole, because it's too cold! When the air temperature drops way below freezing, there's not enough moisture in the air for it to snow. In fact, it's so dry at the South Pole that only a few inches of snow fall annually, which means it is officially classified as a desert. In contrast, Thompson Pass, Alaska, receives an average of 45 feet (14 m) of snow each year.

3. IN 2008 AN UPSIDE-DOWN RAINBOW APPEARED IN THE SKY OVER CAMBRIDGE, ENGLAND.

TRUE

Upside-down or "inverted" rainbows look like smiles in the sky. They are rare, but in 2008 one appeared over Cambridge, England. These upside-down rainbows happen when light bounces off tiny bits of ice that are high up in the sky, reflecting light rays upward instead of downward.

4. COWS CAN PREDICT THE WEATHER.

FALSE

In days of old, before accurate weather forecasts, people relied on signs from nature to predict the weather. One popular belief was that if cows were lying down in a field, rain was coming. While there may be some element of truth in this—it would keep some parts of their bodies dry and the ground beneath them dry—it's far more likely that they are chewing the cud, or partially digested grass, which they regurgitate and chew again. Cows tend to lie down to do this.

5. IN VENEZUELA A SINGLE LIGHTNING STORM RAGED FOR 360 DAYS.

FALSE

No storm has raged for as long as 360 days, but "Catatumbo Lightning" is a phenomenon that occurs on about 160 nights of the year near Lake Maracaibo, in Venezuela. For up to 10 hours, thousands of powerful lightning bolts zigzag through the sky. This amazing spectacle has taken place for thousands of years, and the local fishermen use the lightning to guide them at night, like a lighthouse.

6. BALLS OF FIRE SOMETIMES FLOAT THROUGH THE AIR DURING THUNDERSTORMS.

TRUE

Not much is known about ball lightning because it's difficult to predict when and where it will happen. It appears as glowing spheres of light that float in the air close to ground level, drifting along and sometimes hovering. It isn't surprising that some of these mysterious glowing balls have been mistaken for UFOs.

7. IT CAN RAIN FROGS AND FISH.

TRUE

You've probably heard the expression "It's raining cats and dogs," but did you know that it's possible to get caught in a shower of fish and frogs? Sometimes unlucky aquatic creatures are scooped up into the atmosphere by waterspouts—tornadoes that form over water. As they spin, water is scooped up at the base, carrying wildlife with it. When the waterspouts die down, the animals are dumped, often miles away from their homes.

8. DURING A THUNDERSTORM, STREET LAMPS AND SHIPS' MASTS MAY SPARK BLUE FLAMES THAT CAN'T BE EXTINGUISHED.

TRUE

Some objects, such as airplane wings, street lamps, and ships' masts, may appear to be on fire, but it's actually luminous plasma surrounding an object in an area that is electrically charged during a thunderstorm. The phenomenon is known as St. Elmo's Fire, after Saint Elmo, the patron saint of sailors. Magellan, Caesar, and Columbus all experienced St. Elmo's Fire on their journeys.

Hard Rocks

Earth is full of amazing minerals and rocks, but do you know the hard truth about these gems of information? Mark your answers in the circles provided, then check pages 62–64 to dig up the truth.

THE FACTS	TRUE	FALSE
1. Some rocks can change into a different kind of rock.	○	○
2. Earth's largest crater from a meteorite strike is 328 feet (100 m) wide.	○	○
3. Most metals come from rocks called ores.	○	○
4. Some crystals can grow in a few hours.	○	○
5. Amber is a stone that's made when lava from a volcanic eruption cools rapidly.	○	○
6. Sand and mud are actually tiny rocks.	○	○
7. Trees can turn into stone.	○	○

1. SOME ROCKS CAN CHANGE INTO A DIFFERENT KIND OF ROCK.

TRUE

Some rocks, when they are subject to great heat or pressure deep in the Earth's crust, can, over thousands of years, change into a different type of rock. They are known as metamorphic rocks, which means "change of form." Marble is a hard metamorphic rock that forms from limestone. It is often polished and used in buildings or to make statues.

2. EARTH'S LARGEST CRATER FROM A METEORITE STRIKE IS 328 FEET (100 M) WIDE.

FALSE

The largest crater from a meteorite (an object from outer space) strike is in Vredefort, South Africa. It measures an incredible 186 miles (300 km) across and is more than 2,000 million years old.

3. MOST METALS COME FROM ROCKS CALLED ORES.

TRUE

Some rocks contain minerals that can be mined and processed to extract metals. These are known as ores. An ore known as hematite, for example, produces iron. To produce some metals, an enormous amount of ore needs to be extracted, so the mines can be huge—up to 1 mile (1.5 km) deep.

4. SOME CRYSTALS CAN GROW IN A FEW HOURS.

TRUE

When a liquid cools down and becomes solid, crystals form. In nature this usually happens very slowly, but if you want to see a speedy version, mix equal parts of epsom salts and very hot, but not boiling, water in a shallow bowl. Stir the mixture thoroughly, until no more salts dissolve. Put it in the fridge for three hours and you'll find that the bowl has filled with crystals.

5. AMBER IS A STONE THAT'S MADE WHEN LAVA FROM A VOLCANIC ERUPTION COOLS RAPIDLY.

FALSE

Amber is a substance that has been worn as jewelry for thousands of years. It is sometimes described as a semiprecious stone, even though it is not really a stone at all. It formed over millions of years from fossilized tree resin and often contains perfectly preserved insects, trapped in the sticky resin as it flowed from the trees. Next time you see someone wearing a piece of amber jewelry, take a peek and see if you can spot an insect inside it. The stone that forms when lava thrown from an erupting volcano cools rapidly is actually called pumice.

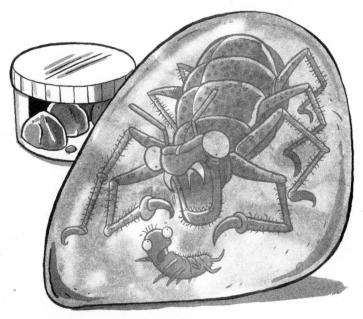

6. SAND AND MUD ARE ACTUALLY TINY ROCKS.

TRUE

Rocks get broken down into smaller pieces over long periods of time by the weather. The small pieces are carried away by the wind and rain and end up at the bottom of rivers and seas as silt, mud, and sand. This is called sediment. Gradually, lots of layers build up and change into a type of rock called sedimentary rock. Over millions of years, the rocks move toward the surface, where they are once again broken into tiny particles. This process is called the rock cycle.

7. TREES CAN TURN INTO STONE.

TRUE

It takes thousands of years for a tree to turn into a fossil. The process is called petrification. It happens when the organic material of the tree is changed to stone. Imagine that thousands of years ago a tree falls on a floodplain and is covered by silt and sediment before it can decompose. Over time, waters flowing through the sediment carry minerals inside the tree, where they replace the organic matter and crystallize. Often, every detail of the tree, including the bark and rings, is preserved by these crystals, so that although the tree has been transformed into a rock, the fossil still looks like a tree.

Ominous Oceans

Oceans are some of the most magnificent places on the planet, but can you fish out the fibs among these facts? Mark your answers, then turn to pages 66–68 for the truth.

THE FACTS	TRUE	FALSE
1. Ships and planes are banned from the Bermuda Triangle because so many have mysteriously disappeared.	◯	◯
2. Red tides are caused when blood from a shark's feeding frenzy washes up on land.	◯	◯
3. There is no life in the ocean beyond depths of 656 feet (200 m).	◯	◯
4. Throwing stones into the sea causes storms and huge waves.	◯	◯
5. Oceans are too salty to freeze.	◯	◯
6. Ocean waters sometimes glow at night.	◯	◯
7. A mouthful of seawater contains millions of living organisms.	◯	◯

1. SHIPS AND PLANES ARE BANNED FROM THE BERMUDA TRIANGLE BECAUSE SO MANY HAVE MYSTERIOUSLY DISAPPEARED.

FALSE

The Bermuda Triangle is a stretch of water in the Atlantic Ocean where more than a hundred ships and six planes have mysteriously disappeared. Some people believe that this unlucky area is cursed or that the missing vessels and their crews were abducted by aliens. Scientists, however, believe that most of the craft have disappeared due to freak weather events, underwater explosions, or planes simply running out of fuel. Whatever the truth, no one is banned from the Bermuda Triangle.

2. RED TIDES ARE CAUSED WHEN BLOOD FROM A SHARK'S FEEDING FRENZY WASHES UP ON LAND.

FALSE

Red tides aren't tides full of blood, and they aren't caused by sharks. In fact, they happen when thousands of tiny red sea creatures (phytoplankton) reproduce quickly, causing a visible red swirl called a "bloom" in the water. The bloom can be harmful to humans and other creatures. When a red tide is spotted, it can be dangerous to swim in the water or eat seafood caught in that area, so warnings are issued.

3. THERE IS NO LIFE IN THE OCEAN BEYOND DEPTHS OF 656 FEET (200 M).

FALSE

Sunlight can't penetrate beyond ocean depths of around 656 feet (200 m), but life still flourishes far below these depths in the "aphotic'" zone. Aphotic means "without light." In 1977 scientists were amazed to find life on the ocean floor at depths of more than 6,561 feet (2,000 m), where shrimp, crabs, and fish were found in the icy pitch-black waters. The creatures were living around hydrothermal vents, which are areas on the seafloor where water heated by magma under the seabed gushes out. The tiny organisms feed off the minerals in the water.

4. THROWING STONES INTO THE SEA CAUSES STORMS AND HUGE WAVES.

FALSE

This is one of the many superstitions sailors believed about the sea. Sailors also thought that whistling would whip up a storm. In reality, waves are caused by the wind, so you don't need to worry about any stones you toss into the waters as you whistle happily on the beach!

5. OCEANS ARE TOO SALTY TO FREEZE.

FALSE

Just like fresh water, seawater can freeze. In fact, at certain times of the year, sea ice actually covers about 15 percent of the world's oceans. While fresh water freezes at a temperature of 32°F (0°C), the salt in seawater means it needs a lower temperature of at least 29°F (−1.9°C) to freeze.

6. OCEAN WATERS SOMETIMES GLOW AT NIGHT.

TRUE

Sometimes, at night, people have reported that the ocean appears to glow with small spots of a strange blue light. This is caused by clusters of tiny living things, called algae, giving off light in a process known as bioluminescence. It happens because of a chemical reaction inside the creature, and when there are millions of these algae gathered in one spot, the ocean can appear to glow. These spots are often seen around boats, as they plough through the water, churning it up.

7. A MOUTHFUL OF SEAWATER CONTAINS MILLIONS OF LIVING ORGANISMS.

TRUE

A mouthful of seawater contains much more than just salt; it holds more than 10 million individual bacteria, which represents over a thousand different species! And there's some larger organisms, too, like 10,000 tiny plants called phytoplankton and hundreds of tiny animals known as zooplankton. But don't worry if you happen to swallow a mouthful or two. Most of these microscopic critters are harmless—and they are packed with protein!

Lethal Landscapes

The world has plenty of places that are harmful to your health if you don't have the equipment and know-how to survive. Decide from the safety of your armchair whether these facts are true or false, then check pages 70–72 to see if you're right.

THE FACTS	TRUE	FALSE
1. Death Valley was named by the only survivor of a doomed journey through it.	O	O
2. The world's fastest tidal bore travels at speeds of up to 25 miles (40 km) per hour.	O	O
3. The Ring of Fire is a dangerous area known for having hundreds of wildfires every year.	O	O
4. In Coober Pedy, Australia, most people live underground because of the heat.	O	O
5. Humans cannot survive in Antarctica without modern technology.	O	O
6. Hundreds of terrible tornadoes tear through Tornado Alley in the United States annually.	O	O

1. DEATH VALLEY WAS NAMED BY THE ONLY SURVIVOR OF A DOOMED JOURNEY THROUGH IT.

FALSE

Death Valley is the hottest, driest place in North America. It is located in the Mojave Desert in eastern California. In 1849 thousands of people in America were heading west, looking for gold. Some members of a wagon train decided to follow a shortcut through the valley. They were trapped there for four months. The group was rescued when two of them headed over the mountains for supplies, then returned to lead everyone to safety. Miraculously, just one of the prospectors died, but as they left the valley, one of them supposedly said, "Good-bye, Death Valley," and the name has stuck ever since.

2. THE WORLD'S FASTEST TIDAL BORE TRAVELS AT SPEEDS OF UP TO 25 MILES (40 KM) PER HOUR.

TRUE

The world's fastest tidal bore (a rush of water that travels upstream from a broad bay into a shallower area or inlet against the direction a river flows) occurs in China's Qiantang River. The water rushes up the river at great speed in a wave that can be up to 30 feet (9 m) high. Even so, a few people have been crazy enough to attempt to surf it.

3. THE RING OF FIRE IS A DANGEROUS AREA KNOWN FOR HAVING HUNDREDS OF WILDFIRES EVERY YEAR.

FALSE

The Ring of Fire is a horseshoe-shaped area around the edges of the Pacific Ocean that stretches for 25,000 miles (40,000 km). It is where 75 percent of the world's volcanoes are found and is the site of frequent earthquakes and volcanic eruptions. Japan sits on the Ring of Fire, and in March 2011 it was hit by one of the most powerful earthquakes on record, with a magnitude of 9.0. This was followed by a devastating tsunami. Just a month before, New Zealand, which also sits on the Ring of Fire, was hit by an earthquake with a magnitude of 6.3.

4. IN COOBER PEDY, AUSTRALIA, MOST PEOPLE LIVE UNDERGROUND BECAUSE OF THE HEAT.

TRUE

Coober Pedy is a town in an area of Australia known as the Outback. Precious stones called opals are mined there. The searing daytime heat makes living there a challenge, so the majority of the town's 4,000 residents live underground in houses carved from the sandstone rocks. There are stores, churches, and even an underground swimming pool, which make life more bearable in temperatures that regularly exceed 104°F (40°C) in the shade.

5. HUMANS CANNOT SURVIVE IN ANTARCTICA WITHOUT MODERN TECHNOLOGY.

TRUE

The majority of people who work in Antarctica are research scientists staying there for a few months at a time. There are no permanent inhabitants. Surviving Antarctica takes careful planning and training. It is made possible by modern technology, which provides the specialty clothing, communication equipment, transportation, and high-energy food needed to live there. Without these, humans would be unable to survive for long—in winter, temperatures can average −76°F (−60°C). Fingers, toes, noses, and ears are all vulnerable to frostbite. The cold stops blood flowing to them, and the flesh freezes and turns black as it dies.

6. HUNDREDS OF TERRIBLE TORNADOES TEAR THROUGH TORNADO ALLEY IN THE UNITED STATES ANNUALLY.

TRUE

Tornado Alley is a nickname given to an area in the southern plains of the central United States. Hundreds of tornadoes cross the region every year, mostly in late spring and early autumn. They are so frequent that some people in the region build underground tornado shelters in their yards to protect them during storms.

Fantastic Formations

From magnificent mountains to riveting reefs, fabulous formations can be found all over the world. Can you tell which of these facts are real? Mark your answers below, then turn to pages 74 and 75 to find out.

THE FACTS	TRUE	FALSE
1. Wave Rock is a cliff on the coast of Australia. During storms, huge waves crash over the top.	○	○
2. The Giant's Causeway in Northern Ireland formed over 50 million years ago when a volcano erupted.	○	○
3. In the Philippines the Chocolate Hills are named after the sweet smell of the cacao trees growing there.	○	○
4. A single crystal in Mexico's Cave of Crystals can measure 6.5 feet (2 m) wide and 36 feet (11 m) long.	○	○
5. The Great Barrier Reef was built by humans.	○	○
6. Cave popcorn is a type of rock that forms in caves.	○	○

1. WAVE ROCK IS A CLIFF ON THE COAST OF AUSTRALIA. DURING STORMS, HUGE WAVES CRASH OVER THE TOP.

FALSE

Australia's Wave Rock isn't on the coast at all. It stands 49 feet (15 m) high and 360 feet (110 m) long, just outside the town of Hyden, Western Australia. The huge granite formation looks like a curling wave that's about to crash onto the ground below. Scientists believe it was created over thousands of years as softer rock beneath the upper edge of the cliff was worn away by the wind and rain.

2. THE GIANT'S CAUSEWAY IN NORTHERN IRELAND FORMED OVER 50 MILLION YEARS AGO WHEN A VOLCANO ERUPTED.

TRUE

Irish legend says that a giant named Finn McCool made the causeway to cross the sea and fight a Scottish giant named Benandonner. In truth this incredible rock formation formed more than 50 million years ago when lava from a volcanic eruption rapidly cooled and cracked to form 40,000 hexagonal (six-sided) columns of basalt rock.

3. IN THE PHILIPPINES THE CHOCOLATE HILLS ARE NAMED AFTER THE SWEET SMELL OF THE CACAO TREES GROWING THERE.

FALSE

The 1,776 unusual dome-shaped hills in Bohol, in the Philippines, are so named because in the dry season the vegetation turns brown and they look like mounds of chocolate. Scientists can't agree on how they formed, and sadly, they don't taste or smell like the real thing!

4. A SINGLE CRYSTAL IN MEXICO'S CAVE OF CRYSTALS CAN MEASURE 6.5 FEET (2 M) WIDE AND 36 FEET (11 M) LONG.

TRUE

In 2000, workers in the Naica mine in Mexico discovered a chamber full of enormous crystals 1,000 feet (300 m) below the Earth's surface. Their beauty has led to it being dubbed the Sistine Chapel of crystals.

5. THE GREAT BARRIER REEF WAS BUILT BY HUMANS.

FALSE

The Great Barrier Reef is made from corals, which are colonies of ocean creatures called polyps. It is the largest living structure on the planet, stretching for more than 1,429 miles (2,300 km) along the

northeast coast of Australia. It has taken thousands of years to grow to its current size. Coral reefs are often called "gardens of the sea" because they teem with ocean life.

6. CAVE POPCORN IS A TYPE OF ROCK THAT FORMS IN CAVES.

TRUE

Cave popcorn forms when water drips on the walls, floors, and ceilings of limestone caves, leaving behind deposits of a mineral called calcite. These knoblike lumps resemble popcorn.

THE SCIENCE
PART

Terrific Technology

Humans have been toying with technology for centuries—from the first tools used by cave dwellers to the latest gadgets. Decide whether the following facts are true or false, then turn to pages 80–82 to see if you know the technological truth.

THE FACTS	TRUE	FALSE
1. The first flush toilet was invented by Thomas Crapper in 1861.	O	O
2. The first bicycle had no pedals.	O	O
3. The first "mobile" phones were too heavy to carry around.	O	O
4. It took eight hours to take the world's first photograph.	O	O
5. The screen on the first television set was more than 78 inches (2 m) wide.	O	O
6. The world's fastest train floats above the tracks.	O	O
7. The first helicopter design was sketched by Leonardo da Vinci in the 15th century.	O	O

1. THE FIRST FLUSH TOILET WAS INVENTED BY THOMAS CRAPPER IN 1861.

FALSE

Many people wrongly believe that a man named Thomas Crapper invented the flush toilet. In fact, its design has been refined over centuries by numerous people. Toilets with a very simple flush system have been found in the ruins of the palace at Knossos, Crete—dating from 4,000 years ago! In 1596 Sir John Harrington built one for Queen Elizabeth I of England. The waste was flushed away through a trapdoor that opened directly into a cesspool. The smell was so awful that it didn't catch on. In 1820 Albert Giblin patented his design for the flush toilet, but it was 37 years before the first toilet paper was sold to go with it!

2. THE FIRST BICYCLE HAD NO PEDALS.

TRUE

One of the first bicycles was invented in 1790. It was made from wood but had no steering or pedals. The rider sat astride it and moved by pushing their feet along the ground. In 1817 Karl Drais improved it with his "running bicycle," which could be steered. A blacksmith named Kirkpatrick MacMillan added pedals in 1839. The design was further improved later that century by the addition of a chain and pneumatic (air-filled) tires, which led to the bicycle becoming safer and very popular.

3. THE FIRST "MOBILE" PHONES WERE TOO HEAVY TO CARRY AROUND.

TRUE

The first mobile phone call was made in 1973, but it was almost a decade before the first handsets went on sale. Early handsets looked like a phone stuck on a car battery. They were very heavy and had a talk time of just 20 minutes. In 1983 the "brick" handset was launched. It got its name because it was as big as a brick and only a little lighter. It cost so much that few people could afford it.

4. IT TOOK EIGHT HOURS TO TAKE THE WORLD'S FIRST PHOTOGRAPH.

TRUE

When Joseph Niépce took the world's first photograph in 1826, it wasn't just a case of "point and shoot," as it is with today's digital cameras. It was a complex process involving a pewter plate coated with chemicals. This was placed in something called a "camera obscura." Light was projected onto a flat surface inside the camera, producing an image of the scene outside. It took eight hours for light to harden the chemicals on the plate. The plate was then washed in more chemicals to reveal the image. Further developments saw a move from plates to film, then to the digital process that is used by cameras today.

5. THE SCREEN ON THE FIRST TELEVISION SET WAS MORE THAN 78 INCHES (2 M) WIDE.

FALSE

John Logie Baird first demonstrated his "televisor" machine in 1926. The screen was not huge. In fact, it was so small that only one person could see the picture at a time, and the image was very weak. At that point, sound could not be transmitted at the same time as the picture.

6. THE WORLD'S FASTEST TRAIN FLOATS ABOVE THE TRACKS.

TRUE

China's Maglev train (the name comes from "magnetic levitation") floats 0.4 inches (1 cm) above the tracks, thanks to electromagnets in the train and tracks. It travels at speeds of up to 267 miles (430 km) per hour.

7. THE FIRST HELICOPTER DESIGN WAS SKETCHED BY LEONARDO DA VINCI IN THE 15TH CENTURY.

TRUE

Leonardo da Vinci was what's known as a Renaissance man, which means that he was interested in everything and was good at most things. He is probably best known as the 15th-century artist who painted the *Mona Lisa,* but the sketches and notebooks he left behind are equally important. Among his sketches are early designs for a helicopter and scuba gear, although it was several centuries before the ideas became reality.

Dramatic Discoveries

Throughout history, dramatic discoveries have been made, and some of them seemed quite shocking at the time. Read the facts below to see if you can uncover the truth, then turn to pages 84–86 to find out if you were right.

THE FACTS	TRUE	FALSE
1. Galileo was arrested and his books banned when he claimed that the Earth revolved around the sun.	○	○
2. Michael Faraday discovered electricity in 1831.	○	○
3. Sir Isaac Newton wrote his theory on the law of gravity after an apple fell on his head.	○	○
4. Watching icebergs led to the theory of continental drift.	○	○
5. Charles Darwin's ideas in his book *On the Origin of Species* were so radical that he delayed publishing them for years.	○	○
6. Fire has been used by humans for more than a million years.	○	○

1. GALILEO WAS ARRESTED AND HIS BOOKS BANNED WHEN HE CLAIMED THAT THE EARTH REVOLVED AROUND THE SUN.

TRUE

Galileo Galilei was a 17th-century Italian astronomer and philosopher who used one of the first telescopes to study the universe. His discoveries supported earlier claims by a man named Copernicus, who believed the planets revolved around the sun. This was seen as a challenge to the Catholic Church, because at the time, the church believed that everything revolved around the Earth. Galileo's claims led to him being tried and found guilty of heresy—which means disagreeing with the beliefs and teachings of the Catholic Church. Galileo was kept under house arrest for the rest of his life.

2. MICHAEL FARADAY DISCOVERED ELECTRICITY IN 1831.

FALSE

People were aware of electricity even in ancient times. But until a man named Faraday discovered that magnetism could produce electricity, which is known as electromagnetic induction, it was considered to be nothing more than a curiosity. Faraday went on to develop an electric motor and generator. His findings made it possible to harness electricity as power for the first time.

3. SIR ISAAC NEWTON WROTE HIS THEORY ON THE LAW OF GRAVITY AFTER AN APPLE FELL ON HIS HEAD.

FALSE

Sir Isaac Newton was one of Britain's most influential scientists. He wrote his theory on the law of gravity in the 17th century, but it doesn't mention an apple hitting him on the head. It's more likely that he had seen one falling from a tree and later anecdotes were embellished to jazz the story up.

4. WATCHING ICEBERGS LED TO THE THEORY OF CONTINENTAL DRIFT.

TRUE

In 1912 Alfred Wegener noticed that on a map, the east coast of South America looked as if it fit into the west coast of Africa, like a jigsaw puzzle. Then one day he was watching icebergs drifting out to sea and realized that the continents must be moving, too. It was not until the 1960s that scientists could prove his theory.

5. CHARLES DARWIN'S IDEAS IN HIS BOOK *ON THE ORIGIN OF SPECIES* WERE SO RADICAL THAT HE DELAYED PUBLISHING THEM FOR YEARS.

TRUE

A scientist named Charles Darwin spent many years on a voyage to study plants and animals. He observed that creatures have to compete with each other for food and shelter. Within each species, certain creatures were born with features that made them more able to survive than others and pass the features on to their young. Over time these features became more common, so the species changed, or "evolved." For example, a moth that was darker than others blended better with dark tree bark. As a result, it was less likely to be eaten by birds and therefore more likely to survive and pass on its darker shade. At this time, many people believed that the world was created by God in seven days. Darwin's ideas were so radical that he spent more than 20 years carefully gathering evidence before he published his theory of "natural selection" in 1859. As he expected, when his ideas were finally published, many people were outraged.

6. FIRE HAS BEEN USED BY HUMANS FOR MORE THAN A MILLION YEARS.

TRUE

Early humans started to use fires that occurred naturally—as a result of lightning strikes or the friction of rock falls—more than 1.5 million years ago. It took a long time before they discovered how to make it. When they found a fire that had started naturally, they would keep the fire going and use it for warmth and food. About 10,000 years ago people discovered how to make fire by striking a flint against a rock called pyrite.

Bonkers Biology

Sometimes the truth about biology is stranger than fiction. But can you tell which facts are real and which are fiendish fakes? Make your choices, then turn to pages 88–90 to find out if you were right.

THE FACTS	TRUE	FALSE
1. The liger and the pizzly bear are examples of crossbred animals.	○	○
2. In the 17th century, boys at a school in Eton, England, were punished if they didn't smoke.	○	○
3. The skeletons of babies and adult humans have the same number of parts.	○	○
4. All forms of bacteria are harmful to humans.	○	○
5. Fruits and vegetables that are super rich in vitamins have been developed by scientists.	○	○
6. No two humans have the same DNA.	○	○
7. Mold is nature's way of recycling.	○	○
8. Coral from the sea can replace bones in the human body.	○	○

Brilliant or bonkers? Turn the page to find out.

1. THE LIGER AND THE PIZZLY BEAR ARE EXAMPLES OF CROSSBRED ANIMALS.

TRUE

Strange as it may seem, some wild animals can be crossbred in captivity. So a lion and tiger may have a baby called a "liger." A "pizzly bear" is a polar bear bred with a grizzly bear. Other hybrids include the zonkey (zebra/donkey), the cama (camal/llama), and the wolpin (whale/dolphin).

2. IN THE 17TH CENTURY, BOYS AT A SCHOOL IN ETON, ENGLAND, WERE PUNISHED IF THEY DIDN'T SMOKE.

TRUE

Nowadays smoking is known to be harmful to health, and any schoolkid caught puffing on a cigarette is likely to be hauled over the coals by their teacher. But in the 17th century, when plague was rife, people noticed that the owners of tobacco shops didn't seem to get sick. So at Eton, a school near London, boys were punished if they didn't smoke pipe tobacco.

3. THE SKELETONS OF BABIES AND ADULT HUMANS HAVE THE SAME NUMBER OF PARTS.

FALSE

When babies are born, their skeletons contain nearly 300 parts. As they grow older, some of the parts fuse together, and by adulthood the skeleton consists of 206 bones.

4. ALL FORMS OF BACTERIA ARE HARMFUL TO HUMANS.

FALSE

Bacteria are microscopic single-celled organisms. They are found everywhere, even inside our bodies. Some bacteria are helpful to humans. For example, within our colons there are more than 500 different species of bacteria that help to keep us healthy and digest food. They also fight the harmful bacteria that can make us sick.

5. FRUITS AND VEGETABLES THAT ARE SUPER RICH IN VITAMINS HAVE BEEN DEVELOPED BY SCIENTISTS.

TRUE

Scientists have started to develop genetically modified crops (GM crops) that are resistant to disease and give higher yields. They are also working on genetically modified fruits and vegetables, mostly to help them stay fresher longer and to improve the taste. It's in its early days, but so far, purple tomatoes have been created that are rich in chemicals said to prevent cancer. Scientists are also working to produce "edible vaccines" in bananas, but it will be a while before they appear on our tables. There is a lot of debate around the science of GM food. Many people aren't eager to eat it, and they worry about the unknown negative effects of eating GM food over many years.

6. NO TWO HUMANS HAVE THE SAME DNA.

FALSE

A chemical called DNA is contained in each cell of your body. It acts as a chemical code of instructions telling your body how to grow. It is inherited from your parents. Each person's DNA is unique, except for the DNA of identical twins. These twins grow from the same egg, which splits to form the two embryos that will grow into two babies. Each embryo contains the same DNA, which is why identical twins often look alike. There are some differences, though; identical twins have similar, but not identical, fingerprints.

7. MOLD IS NATURE'S WAY OF RECYCLING.

TRUE

Mold is a type of fungus. It grows from tiny particles, or "spores," floating in the air. Mold is useful in nature because it helps to get rid of organic matter, such as fruits, vegetables, and leaves, by rotting it and returning it to the soil. The downside of mold is that because it destroys the things it grows on, when it grows in homes, it can be a real problem. It can mess up walls and furniture. Sometimes it can make people sick, since the spores can cause allergies, asthma attacks, and even chest infections.

8. CORAL FROM THE SEA CAN REPLACE BONES IN THE HUMAN BODY.

TRUE

The chemistry of coral is so close to human bones that it is being used to repair or replace them. To repair a fracture, doctors inject treated coral that's been formed into a paste. After a couple of hours, the paste dries and is as hard as the human bone and melds almost seamlessly with the human skeleton. In fact, this alternative treatment has become so effective that it may completely replace traditional metal plates, pins, and screws someday.

90

Out of This World

The universe is still mostly unexplored, but scientists have made some pretty impressive discoveries. Look at the facts below to decide which ones are true. Then turn to pages 92–94 to find out the truth.

THE FACTS	TRUE	FALSE
1. Four planets in the solar system are made of just gas and liquid.	○	○
2. Mercury, which is closest to the sun, is always hot.	○	○
3. Jupiter's Red Spot is a huge storm that's been raging for more than 300 years.	○	○
4. Years ago people used to believe that the moon was made of cheese.	○	○
5. Shooting stars are dying stars falling from the sky.	○	○
6. The first animals to survive a mission in space were monkeys.	○	○
7. Nothing, not even light, can escape from a black hole.	○	○
8. The sun makes up only 10 percent of the solar system's mass.	○	○

1. FOUR PLANETS IN THE SOLAR SYSTEM ARE MADE OF JUST GAS AND LIQUID.

TRUE

The four planets closest to the Sun are Mercury, Venus, Earth, and Mars. They are composed of rock. Farther away from the sun, the planets Jupiter, Saturn, Uranus, and Neptune are known as "gas giants." Scientists believe that they are made up of a molten core similar to Earth's, surrounded by a thick layer of gas rather than a solid surface. If, one day, technology allows us to reach these planets, spacecraft probably won't be able to land on them.

2. MERCURY, WHICH IS CLOSEST TO THE SUN, IS ALWAYS HOT.

FALSE

The temperature of the part of Mercury that is facing the sun at any one time is exceptionally hot, reaching around 486°F (252°C). Temperatures on the dark side of the planet can plummet to lows of −297°F (−183°C). Now that's chilly!

3. JUPITER'S RED SPOT IS A HUGE STORM THAT'S BEEN RAGING FOR MORE THAN 300 YEARS.

TRUE

The Great Red Spot is a spot on the surface of Jupiter. It is twice the size of Earth. It is actually a violent storm that has been raging for centuries. In 2006 another, smaller red storm appeared. It is known as Oval BA or Red Junior.

4. YEARS AGO PEOPLE USED TO BELIEVE THAT THE MOON WAS MADE OF CHEESE.

FALSE

Nobody ever believed the moon was made of cheese despite the expression—"The moon is made of green cheese"—that dates back almost 500 years. It means that something is so absurd that no one would possibly believe it was true. Green cheese in this case meant unripened cheese rather than the moldy variety.

5. SHOOTING STARS ARE DYING STARS FALLING FROM THE SKY.

FALSE

Shooting stars are not stars at all, but meteors, or pieces of rock, hurtling through space. Some of them hit the top of Earth's atmosphere and burn up in the heat. They glow brightly for a few moments as they streak across the sky. When lots of shooting stars are seen together, they form what's known as a meteor shower. If you are lucky enough to see one, make a wish!

6. THE FIRST ANIMALS TO SURVIVE A MISSION IN SPACE WERE MONKEYS.

TRUE

In 1959 two tiny monkeys, named Able and Baker, survived a mission in space. Their flight, which reached speeds of 10,000 miles (16,090 km) per hour, lasted just 15 minutes. The monkeys survived the mission, although Able died shortly after. Since then a host of animals, such as frogs, dogs, and even worms have been sent into space.

7. NOTHING, NOT EVEN LIGHT, CAN ESCAPE FROM A BLACK HOLE.

TRUE

A star known as a "giant star" can undergo a massive explosion, known as a supernova, at the end of its life. Sometimes the star collapses in on itself. If this happens, a black hole forms. The force of gravity is so strong inside a black hole that everything nearby, even light, gets sucked into it and cannot escape.

8. THE SUN MAKES UP ONLY 10 PERCENT OF THE SOLAR SYSTEM'S MASS.

FALSE

The sun actually makes up more than 99 percent of the solar system's mass! That means that all the planets put together, as well as all the asteroids, make up the rest. Although it looks like just a big round yellow ball of hot gases, the sun has 333,400 times more mass than the Earth. The light we see from the sun comes from just the top 0.1 percent and takes about 8 minutes to reach us. However, radiation from its core takes about 170,000 years to make its way out to the surface, due to the high density of the mass it must travel through!

Weird Science

Brilliant as they are, some scientific experiments and discoveries seem too wacky to be true. Can you uncover the weird truth from these facts? Turn to pages 96–98 to find out what's true and what's not.

THE FACTS	TRUE	FALSE
1. The microwave was invented when a chocolate bar melted in a scientist's pocket.	○	○
2. One of the 20th century's biggest scientific discoveries was an elaborate hoax.	○	○
3. When the Hubble Telescope was first launched, it didn't work.	○	○
4. A vengeful scientist tried to destroy the world's computers with the Y2K virus.	○	○
5. Penicillin was discovered by accident.	○	○
6. When a low-tack glue was invented, at first no one could think of a use for it.	○	○
7. Scientists have reproduced the Big Bang in a lab.	○	○

Is it mad, bad science or is it all true?

1. THE MICROWAVE WAS INVENTED WHEN A CHOCOLATE BAR MELTED IN A SCIENTIST'S POCKET.

TRUE

In 1946 scientist Percy Spencer was checking a piece of equipment called a magnetron, which is the power tube in a radar machine. As he stood in front of it, a bar of chocolate in his pocket began to melt. Later he asked for a bag of corn kernels and held it near the magnetron. His hunch was right—the kernels exploded into puffy white popcorn! From this experiment the microwave oven was born.

2. ONE OF THE 20TH CENTURY'S BIGGEST SCIENTIFIC DISCOVERIES WAS AN ELABORATE HOAX.

TRUE

In 1912 a skull was unearthed in Piltdown, England. Scientists were very excited by the find, since it seemed to be the skull of an early human. The fact that it was found next to what seemed to be a prehistoric cricket bat should have aroused suspicion, but it wasn't until 1953 that it was proved to be an elaborate hoax. An ape's jaw had been attached to a human skull, then aged with chemicals.

3. WHEN THE HUBBLE TELESCOPE WAS FIRST LAUNCHED, IT DIDN'T WORK.

TRUE

The Hubble Telescope was launched in 1990. It cost $2 billion to make, but the first pictures it sent back were useless. Investigations discovered that the curve of the telescope's huge mirror was off by less than a fiftieth of the width of a human hair. As a result, the pictures it produced were blurred. During a daring spacewalk, astronauts attached mirrors to fix it, allowing Hubble to send back incredible images of the universe.

4. A VENGEFUL SCIENTIST TRIED TO DESTROY THE WORLD'S COMPUTERS WITH THE Y2K VIRUS.

FALSE

The Y2K bug was a glitch in computer programs, where the first two digits of the year were fixed at "19." This wasn't a problem until scientists realized that at midnight on December 31, 1999, the computers would return to 1900. People feared that the bug would cause computer failures and chaos. The programs were rewritten, and 2000 arrived without mishap.

5. PENICILLIN WAS DISCOVERED BY ACCIDENT.

TRUE

A substance called penicillin is one of medicine's most important discoveries, but it was actually found by accident. In 1928 scientist Alexander Fleming noticed that a bacterial culture growing in a Petri dish in his lab was contaminated with mold. Around the mold there was no bacteria. Thankfully, Fleming decided to investigate. His discovery led to the birth of penicillin, the world's first antibiotic, which has saved countless lives.

6. WHEN A LOW-TACK GLUE WAS INVENTED, AT FIRST NO ONE COULD THINK OF A USE FOR IT.

TRUE

When Stephen Silver invented a not-very-sticky peelable glue, he couldn't think of a use for it and felt like a failure. Luckily, his colleague, Art Fry, suggested using it on small strips of paper as a place marker in a book, and in 1980 the Post-it note was born.

7. SCIENTISTS HAVE REPRODUCED THE BIG BANG IN A LAB.

FALSE

The Big Bang is the name given to events that occurred during the early development of the universe. The Large Hadron Collider (LHC) tries to re-create the conditions that existed shortly after the Big Bang rather than the moment itself. It isn't kept in a traditional science lab; the LHC is enormous. It is housed in a circular tunnel that runs for 16.5 miles (27 km) under Switzerland.

Curious Cures

In the past, many weird and wacky medical practices were common. Examine the facts below and give your diagnosis, then turn to pages 100–102 for your results.

THE FACTS	TRUE	FALSE
1. In the Stone Age some illnesses were "cured" by drilling a hole in the patient's skull.	○	○
2. Maggots and leeches help healing.	○	○
3. In the past, operations were performed without reliable pain relief.	○	○
4. Today no one believes that people get sick because of evil spirits.	○	○
5. In times of plague, doctors wore bird masks.	○	○
6. Medieval barbers performed surgery and dentistry.	○	○

1. IN THE STONE AGE SOME ILLNESSES WERE "CURED" BY DRILLING A HOLE IN THE PATIENT'S SKULL.

TRUE

"Trepanning" was a form of Stone Age surgery where a hole was drilled with a flint chisel into the head of an unfortunate patient. Scientists can't be certain, but they think that it may have been done to let out what people then believed to be "evil spirits" trapped in the brain of a person who was mentally ill, or possibly to cure a headache before painkillers were developed.

2. MAGGOTS AND LEECHES HELP HEALING.

TRUE

You may be surprised to hear that maggots and leeches still play a part in medicine today. Maggots have been used for hundreds of years as a method of cleaning wounds. They eat only dead or rotting tissue, leaving healthy flesh untouched, so they are great for helping wounds heal. Leeches were used originally to suck out "bad blood," and although there's no scientific basis for this, they do produce a chemical that prevents blood from clotting. Applying leeches to a wound site increases the blood flow to the area, which aids recovery. The only thing patients have to overcome is the yuck factor!

3. IN THE PAST, OPERATIONS WERE PERFORMED WITHOUT RELIABLE PAIN RELIEF.

TRUE

Before 1846, patients undergoing operations suffered dreadful agony. They often died from shock or infection after surgery, and the only way to minimize suffering was to operate as quickly as possible while the patient was held down. In 1846 a substance called ether was used by Robert Liston. Patients slept and felt no pain. Chloroform was subsequently used, but it was better hygiene that really increased a patient's chances of recovery.

4. TODAY NO ONE BELIEVES THAT PEOPLE GET SICK BECAUSE OF EVIL SPIRITS.

FALSE

Doctors have accepted for a long time that most illnesses are caused by bacteria and viruses, not evil spirits. However, in some parts of the world, people still believe that some illnesses are caused by evil spirits attacking the person. In the Voodoo religion, the idea of spirit and healing is central. If spirits are not respected, people believe they will cause problems.

5. IN TIMES OF PLAGUE, DOCTORS WORE BIRD MASKS.

TRUE

Plague wiped out millions of people during epidemics. The worst was the Black Death, which struck several times during the 14th century and killed more than 25 million people in Europe alone. During times of plague, people known as "plague doctors" wore terrifying bird masks with hollow beaks stuffed full of herbs and flowers. They believed that these would protect the wearer from catching the disease. The masks also protected them from the terrible smell of the plague victims.

6. MEDIEVAL BARBERS PERFORMED SURGERY AND DENTISTRY.

TRUE

The red-and-white pole outside a barber's shop symbolizes bloodletting, one of the many medical procedures barbers used to perform. In 1540 things began to change, and a law was passed that decreed that British barbers must not carry out any kind of surgery, apart from pulling teeth.

Ingenious Inventions

There are millions of brilliant gadgets that make life a little easier, but some inventions are so crazy they can't be real—or can they? Try to spot the fakes from the facts and check pages 104 and 105 to see if you were right.

THE FACTS	TRUE	FALSE
1. The Japanese word *chindogu* means "most useful invention."	◯	◯
2. You can make ice cream by rolling a ball around.	◯	◯
3. You can buy removable tattoo sleeves.	◯	◯
4. The Uno is a one-wheeled motorcycle.	◯	◯
5. In Japan a toilet for fish has been developed.	◯	◯
6. Doggles are sunglasses for dogs.	◯	◯

1. THE JAPANESE WORD *CHINDOGU* MEANS "MOST USEFUL INVENTION."

FALSE

While many of the world's most bizarre inventions come from Japan, *chindogu* refers to the process of inventing an everyday gadget that solves a problem, but in turn is so embarrassing or tricky to use that it is almost useless. Examples of *chindogu* include mini umbrellas to be worn on the toes of your shoes and a hay fever hat—essentially a toilet roll dispenser worn on your head.

2. YOU CAN MAKE ICE CREAM BY ROLLING A BALL AROUND.

TRUE

What could be nicer than a little exercise followed by some ice cream? It's easy with a special plastic ball. You pour yummy ingredients, plus some ice and salt, into the spaces inside the ball. Throw and catch the ball for 20 minutes until your chilly treat is ready to enjoy.

3. YOU CAN BUY REMOVABLE TATTOO SLEEVES.

TRUE

If you're too young for a tattoo, or if you're old enough and always wanted one but are too scared of the pain, try fake tattoo sleeves. The flesh-colored nylon sleeves come decorated with a selection of designs. The cuffs can be covered up with bracelets or watches. Best of all, if you get tired of them, you can take them off!

4. THE UNO IS A ONE-WHEELED MOTORCYCLE.

FALSE

At first glance the Uno looks like a unicycle crossed with a motorcycle, with one wheel. Actually, it has two wheels that sit side by side. The flick of a switch can transform it into a traditional motorcycle.

5. IN JAPAN A TOILET FOR FISH HAS BEEN DEVELOPED.

FALSE

There's no such thing as a toilet for fish, but there is a toilet with a built-in fish tank. The transparent cistern was designed in China for people who don't have much room for pets. It is perfectly safe for the fish, since the aquarium water in which they swim is in a separate tank.

6. DOGGLES ARE SUNGLASSES FOR DOGS.

TRUE

It's the latest "must have" doggy fashion item. These doggy sunglasses don't mist up, don't let in insects or flies, and provide protection from the sun's dangerous rays.

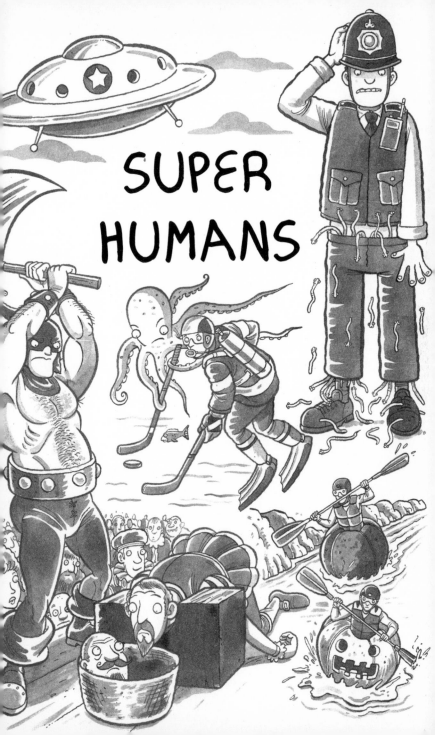

Amazing Ancients

Centuries ago, during ancient times, some pretty amazing things took place. Some of them were advanced, while others seem very odd today. But which are real and which are fake? Make your choices and check your answers on pages 110–112.

THE FACTS	TRUE	FALSE
1. Like the Egyptians, the Aztecs built pyramids to use as royal tombs.	O	O
2. Ancient Greece was the first country to hold the Olympic Games.	O	O
3. The Phoenicians were the first people to record things by writing them down.	O	O
4. The Egyptians mummified their dead to stop them from smelling.	O	O
5. The first farmland in ancient Britain was called the Fertile Crescent.	O	O
6. The Romans had an amazingly advanced plumbing system.	O	O

1. LIKE THE EGYPTIANS, THE AZTECS BUILT PYRAMIDS TO USE AS ROYAL TOMBS.

FALSE

The Aztecs lived in what is now Mexico. Their civilization flourished until the arrival of Spanish conquerors, known as the *conquistadors*, in the 16th century. While it is true that, like the Egyptians, the Aztecs built huge, pyramid-like, stepped structures known as ziggurats, these were not tombs. They towered above the buildings below them, and their steps led to flat tops, on which temples stood. These temples were used in the worship of the Aztec gods. Priests offered human sacrifices to the gods, ripping the heart from the victim's chest.

2. ANCIENT GREECE WAS THE FIRST COUNTRY TO HOLD THE OLYMPIC GAMES.

TRUE

The first recorded Olympic Games were held in 776 B.C., with just one event—a running race. The Games were then held every four years with other events, such as wrestling and chariot racing, added later. The Roman emperor Theodosius I abolished them around A.D. 400. The next Games were held almost 1,500 years later, in 1896.

3. THE PHOENICIANS WERE THE FIRST PEOPLE TO RECORD THINGS BY WRITING THEM DOWN.

FALSE

Many ancient civilizations used early forms of writing to keep records. They were useful to keep track of practical things, such as the crops they were growing. The Sumerians were using symbols to represent letters as early as 3,000 B.C. Their form of writing is known as cuneiform. Ancient Egyptians used hieroglyphics—picture symbols standing for words and sounds. The Phoenicians were the first to use a system of writing that is similar to our own, with sounds being represented by symbols and different symbols being combined to make words. This writing was the basis of the alphabet we use today.

4. THE EGYPTIANS MUMMIFIED THEIR DEAD TO STOP THEM FROM SMELLING.

FALSE

The Egyptians believed that when people died, they lived again in the afterlife. To do this, they needed their body, so it was mummified, or preserved, then laid to rest in a burial chamber inside a tomb. Some kings and queens built huge pyramids to be buried in. As well as the body, the structures housed everything the person would need in the afterlife—from furniture to food and drink.

5. THE FIRST FARMLAND IN ANCIENT BRITAIN WAS CALLED THE FERTILE CRESCENT.

FALSE

The Fertile Crescent is a region now made up of Iraq, Syria, Lebanon, and Israel. Scientists believe that it was the first place in the world where crops were cultivated. After the Ice Age it had a warm, wet climate with fertile soil, so crops grew well. Two rivers, the Euphrates and the Tigris, were close by, so crops could also be watered. The first farmers grew crops from the seeds collected from wild grain, as well as fruits and vegetables. They also raised animals. Gradually, farming spread through Europe and Asia, and civilizations began to flourish.

6. THE ROMANS HAD AN AMAZINGLY ADVANCED PLUMBING SYSTEM.

TRUE

The Romans liked to keep clean, and bathing was a sociable pastime. Roman cities had public baths where people would bathe together. The baths were made possible by the Romans' amazing plumbing system. Clean, fresh water was carried into towns and cities from streams via aqueducts—bridges or tunnels that channeled the water at a steady pace from its source. At the baths the water flowed in through lead pipes. Some rooms were also heated with an under-floor heating system, and sewers carried waste away, dumping it into rivers. After the Roman Empire declined, people returned to their previous filthy ways. Many centuries passed before plumbing became popular once again.

Heroes and Heroines

History is chock-full of daring heroes and brave heroines, but can you tell which of the statements below are heroic facts? Check the circles, then turn to pages 114–116 to find out what's true and what's not.

THE FACTS	TRUE	FALSE
1. Susan B. Anthony was arrested for voting in an election when women couldn't vote.	○	○
2. George Washington seriously considered an offer to become king of the United States.	○	○
3. Marie Curie is the only woman who's been awarded two Nobel prizes.	○	○
4. Mahatma Gandhi helped an entire nation gain independence through peace.	○	○
5. Florence Nightingale was known as the Lady with the Lamp because she brought light to thousands of people.	○	○
6. Harriet Tubman helped hundreds of slaves escape via the Underground Railroad.	○	○
7. An unidentified American serviceman from World War I is buried in the Tomb of the Unknowns.	○	○

1. SUSAN B. ANTHONY WAS ARRESTED FOR VOTING IN AN ELECTION WHEN WOMEN COULDN'T VOTE.

TRUE

Susan B. Anthony, who fought for the rights of women—including the right to vote—was arrested on November 18, 1872, because she voted in the 1872 presidential election at a time when women were not allowed to vote. She was tried and convicted seven months later and ordered to pay a $100 fine. She refused to pay the fine and continued fighting for women's suffrage. She died fourteen years before the 19th amendment (also known as the Susan B. Anthony amendment) was passed in 1920, giving women the right to vote.

2. GEORGE WASHINGTON SERIOUSLY CONSIDERED AN OFFER TO BECOME KING OF THE UNITED STATES.

FALSE

Although Lewis Nicola, a colonel in the Continental army, wrote Washington a letter in 1782 suggesting that Washington consider becoming a king in the new government, Washington was offended by the idea and immediately rejected it. He believed in civilian rule and completely supported the Declaration of Independence. Nicola apologized to Washington several times for bringing up the idea.

3. MARIE CURIE IS THE ONLY WOMAN WHO'S BEEN AWARDED TWO NOBEL PRIZES.

TRUE

Marie Curie was a scientist whose research into radioactivity led to the use of X-rays in medicine. She was awarded the Nobel Prize for Physics in 1903 and for Chemistry in 1911. She is the only woman to have been awarded the Nobel Prize twice.

4. MAHATMA GANDHI HELPED AN ENTIRE NATION GAIN INDEPENDENCE THROUGH PEACE.

TRUE

Mohandas Gandhi is often known as Mahatma, which means "great soul." He was an inspirational man who brought about social and political change in India and greatly helped the poor. He inspired fellow Indians to use peaceful protest to try to gain independence from Britain. Gandhi also tried to stop Hindus and Muslims from fighting each other, but in 1948 he was murdered.

5. FLORENCE NIGHTINGALE WAS KNOWN AS THE LADY WITH THE LAMP BECAUSE SHE BROUGHT LIGHT TO THOUSANDS OF PEOPLE.

FALSE

In 1854 Florence Nightingale was an English nurse who was asked to go to a military hospital in Scutari, Turkey, during the Crimean War. Conditions at the hospital were shocking—overcrowded and dirty. Most of the soldiers there were dying from disease rather than as a result of their wounds. Florence worked tirelessly to improve conditions and often walked the hospital at night, with her lamp in hand, checking on her patients. This is how she came to be called the Lady of the Lamp. Florence Nightingale made nursing a respected profession, and many of today's modern practices are based on her thoughts and ideas.

6. HARRIET TUBMAN HELPED HUNDREDS OF SLAVES ESCAPE VIA THE UNDERGROUND RAILROAD.

TRUE

The Underground Railroad was a network of people who helped slaves escape to freedom. From 1810 to 1850, more than 100,000 southern slaves escaped using this network. When one slave, Harriet Tubman, ran away from her plantation owner in 1849, she fled to the North, where slavery was banned. But Harriet risked her life on 19 occasions, returning south to help more than 300 slaves. She was known to many as Moses because, like Moses in the Bible, she guided slaves to freedom.

7. AN UNIDENTIFIED AMERICAN SERVICEMAN FROM WORLD WAR I IS BURIED IN THE TOMB OF THE UNKNOWNS.

TRUE

On November 11, 1921, this serviceman was buried in the new tomb at Arlington National Cemetery. Later, unidentified servicemen from World War II, the Korean War, and the Vietnam War were buried at the Tomb of the Unknowns, which is also known as the Tomb of the Unknown Soldier (even though it has never been officially named).

Mad, Bad, and Dangerous to Know

You may have heard of some real-life superheroes, but there have also been some folks throughout history that you definitely wouldn't want to meet! See if you can spot the falsehoods about these shady characters, then check pages 118–120 to discover the truth.

THE FACTS	TRUE	FALSE
1. Genghis Khan had molten silver poured into the eyes and ears of an enemy.	○	○
2. Ivan IV of Russia was known as Ivan the Terrible.	○	○
3. Al Capone was finally brought to trial, on charges of tax evasion.	○	○
4. A Hungarian countess bathed in the blood of young girls to keep her skin youthful.	○	○
5. Jack the Ripper was a murderer who was hanged for his crimes in 1888.	○	○
6. Attila the Hun, a ferocious warrior, was finished off by a nosebleed.	○	○

1. GENGHIS KHAN HAD MOLTEN SILVER POURED INTO THE EYES AND EARS OF AN ENEMY.

TRUE

Genghis Khan was a mighty leader who built the biggest empire in the world during the 12th century. He was ruthless with his enemies. When Genghis Khan captured Inalchuq, a governor of an enemy state, he used this gruesome method to kill him.

2. IVAN IV OF RUSSIA WAS KNOWN AS IVAN THE TERRIBLE.

TRUE

Ivan IV was the first tsar of Russia. He was known as Ivan the Terrible because he was incredibly cruel. He created a huge Russian empire in the 16th century but ruled his people with an iron fist. His wild temper led to him to beating his own son to death in a moment of uncontrollable rage.

3. AL CAPONE WAS FINALLY BROUGHT TO TRIAL, ON CHARGES OF TAX EVASION.

TRUE

From the early 1920s to 1931, Al Capone ran a gang in Chicago that was involved in gambling, smuggling liquor, and other illegal activities. He was the mastermind behind the St. Valentine's Day Massacre, when seven men were killed, and was reputed to have ordered the murders of hundreds of others. Yet Capone wasn't convicted of any of these crimes; instead, he was eventually convicted of income-tax evasion and sent to jail.

4. A HUNGARIAN COUNTESS BATHED IN THE BLOOD OF YOUNG GIRLS TO KEEP HER SKIN YOUTHFUL.

FALSE

Countess Elizabeth Bathory of Hungary is said to have been very cruel, but no one can say for certain if the rumor that she bathed in the blood of young girls is true. According to accounts from witnesses at that time, she did kidnap and torture hundreds of girls with the help of her servants, until her vile crimes were discovered. During a raid on her castle in 1609, men reported that they found many girls dead or dying and others held in cells, awaiting beatings or worse. Bathory was imprisoned in her family castle for the rest of her life.

5. JACK THE RIPPER WAS A MURDERER WHO WAS HANGED FOR HIS CRIMES IN 1888.

FALSE

Jack the Ripper was the nickname of a murderer who stalked the streets of London. He brutally killed five women but was never caught. His identity remains a mystery to this day. He was given his nickname after the police received a letter supposedly written by the murderer and signed, "Jack the Ripper." Many books have been written on the subject of the man who literally got away with murder, but his true identity may never be known.

6. ATTILA THE HUN, A FEROCIOUS WARRIOR, WAS FINISHED OFF BY A NOSEBLEED.

TRUE

Attila the Hun was a fearsome warrior and ruler, renowned for his vicious treatment of his enemies. Ironically, in spite of his terrifying reputation, he wasn't killed in battle. He reportedly died at his own wedding in A.D. 453. It is said that he had too much to drink, passed out, and choked to death on blood that spewed from a nosebleed.

Exotic Explorers

Over the years, explorers have embarked on intrepid travels to find uncharted territory. But can you pick out the traveling truths? Turn to pages 122–124 to see if you were heading in the right direction or totally lost.

THE FACTS	TRUE	FALSE
1. Captain Cook died in Hawaii.	○	○
2. A Viking explorer reached North America 500 years before Columbus.	○	○
3. The first explorer to reach the South Pole was Robert Falcon Scott.	○	○
4. Sir Walter Raleigh tried to colonize America.	○	○
5. The first attempt to conquer Mount Everest was made in 1953.	○	○
6. In South America, Spanish explorers found El Dorado, the lost city of gold.	○	○

1. CAPTAIN COOK DIED IN HAWAII.

TRUE

In the 18th century, Captain Cook made three daring voyages, during which he saw many countries that were new to Europeans, including Australia, New Zealand, and the coast of Antarctica. In 1779 he set sail on his third voyage and reached Hawaii. At first Cook and his crew were welcomed, but after a while, there was friction with the islanders, which ultimately led to Cook's being stabbed to death.

2. A VIKING EXPLORER REACHED NORTH AMERICA 500 YEARS BEFORE COLUMBUS.

TRUE

Around the year 1000, Leif Eriksson, son of the Viking warrior Erik the Red, was blown off course while sailing from Greenland to Norway. Stories refer to him arriving in a place he called Vinland. There is evidence of a Viking settlement in what is now Newfoundland, Canada, which matches descriptions of Vinland, so it appears Columbus may have been 500 years too late!

3. THE FIRST EXPLORER TO REACH THE SOUTH POLE WAS ROBERT FALCON SCOTT.

FALSE

In 1912, when Robert Falcon Scott made a grueling trek to the South Pole, he found himself in a race with a team of Norwegians, led by Roald Amundsen. Both men were determined to reach the Pole first. When Scott's team finally reached their target, to their dismay they found the Norwegians had beaten them to it—by a month. On the return journey, Scott and his team perished from starvation and frostbite.

4. SIR WALTER RALEIGH TRIED TO COLONIZE AMERICA.

TRUE

Sir Walter Raleigh is one of England's best-known explorers. In the 16th century, England's queen, Elizabeth I, granted Raleigh permission to colonize America to make England more powerful and wealthy. Raleigh provided financial backing for the first voyage in 1585, and a colony was established at Roanoke Island in what's now North Carolina. It was very short-lived. The settlers were poorly equipped and returned to Britain in 1586.

5. THE FIRST ATTEMPT TO CONQUER MOUNT EVEREST WAS MADE IN 1953.

FALSE

The imposing peak called Mount Everest lies in a mountain range known as the Himalayas. Seven expeditions to climb to the summit, the first in 1922, were unsuccessful. In 1953, when Sir Edmund Hillary and his Sherpa mountain guide, Tenzing Norgay, set out to conquer Everest, no one was sure if it was possible. Hillary and Norgay spent hours battling the bad weather and ferocious winds that whip across the mountain. When they reached the top, Hillary famously said that they could see "the whole world spread out below us."

6. IN SOUTH AMERICA, SPANISH EXPLORERS FOUND EL DORADO, THE LOST CITY OF GOLD.

FALSE

When Spanish explorers heard tales of a mythical lost city made of gold, they were determined to find the place known as El Dorado. Many searched, but it was never found. This legend probably arose from stories of a tribal ceremony. A new king would be covered in gold, making him a "gilded man" or "El Dorado." It's possible these stories were exaggerated over time to become the legend of a city of gold.

Man-Made Madness

Some of the things humans have created are really amazing, while others are just plain crazy. Can you tell which of these facts are true and which are utter nonsense? Mark your answers below, then turn to pages 126–128 to find out which is which.

THE FACTS	TRUE	FALSE
1. In Florida, divers can stay in a hotel 21 feet (6 m) under water.	○	○
2. Diamonds can be grown in a lab.	○	○
3. In Holland there is a museum located inside a human body.	○	○
4. In the 1940s the American military developed a flying saucer.	○	○
5. Scientists have successfully created artificial life.	○	○
6. In Dubai a star-shaped island has been built.	○	○

1. IN FLORIDA, DIVERS CAN STAY IN A HOTEL 21 FEET (6 M) UNDER WATER.

TRUE

Jules's Undersea Lodge in Florida rests 21 feet (6 m) below the surface, at the bottom of a lagoon. Guests scuba dive down to the entrance and step into the lodge through a small, open pool in the wet room. There, they can have a shower and dry off, then relax in the living spaces. Compressed air is pumped into the lodge to stop it from filling with water. There's a living room, bedrooms, and huge round windows through which guests can watch the underwater wildlife.

2. DIAMONDS CAN BE GROWN IN A LAB.

TRUE

Scientists first discovered how to grow, or "culture," synthetic diamonds in the 1950s. Since then, technological advances have led to labs growing diamonds to sell for jewelry and other purposes. Cultured diamonds are real in the sense that they are made of carbon, just like natural diamonds that take millions of years to form. The difference is that cultured diamonds can be grown in just a few days.

3. IN HOLLAND THERE IS A MUSEUM LOCATED INSIDE A HUMAN BODY.

FALSE

You won't find the Corpus Museum in Holland inside a real human body. However, it *is* built inside a giant replica of the human body. Inside, visitors take an interactive journey though the body. You can be a red blood cell, step inside a mouth, and even poke around in a replica of the brain.

4. IN THE 1940S THE AMERICAN MILITARY DEVELOPED A FLYING SAUCER.

FALSE

It wasn't a flying saucer; it was an experimental plane that looked a little like one, designed by Charles Zimmerman, an aeronautical engineer. Although it had a saucerlike shape, it still had wings and propellers. The idea was that it would fly at great speeds and be able to make short landings on aircraft carriers. The U.S. Navy was so impressed that two prototypes were built. However, with the arrival of the jet engine, propeller planes became less popular and the project was abandoned. You could say that the idea never really took off!

5. SCIENTISTS HAVE SUCCESSFULLY CREATED ARTIFICIAL LIFE.

TRUE

In a laboratory in Maryland, Dr. Craig Venter became the first biologist to create artificial life. He constructed a bacteria from new DNA. It is based on an existing bacteria but uses genetic information constructed in the laboratory. It has been named Synthia, because of its synthetic origin, and its DNA contains a special watermark to show that it is artificial.

6. IN DUBAI A STAR-SHAPED ISLAND HAS BEEN BUILT.

FALSE

While it is true that three man-made islands have been constructed in Dubai, they are in the shape of three giant palms, not stars. The islands are called Jumeirah, Jebel Ali, and Deira. Jumeirah is home to an expensive hotel and luxury apartments, as well as restaurants, shops, and leisure facilities.

Brilliant Bodies

The human body does some wonderful and some truly disgusting things. But how well do you know your body? Scan through the facts below and make your choices, then turn to pages 130–132 to see if you were right.

THE FACTS	TRUE	FALSE
1. The human nose produces a cupful of mucus every day.	○	○
2. Your ears help you keep your balance.	○	○
3. Double-jointed people are very bendy because they have extra joints.	○	○
4. Smelly foods make you fart.	○	○
5. Head lice can jump from one human head to another.	○	○
6. Bad breath comes from not cleaning your teeth.	○	○
7. There can be up to 10 million bacteria on a human hand.	○	○

1. THE HUMAN NOSE PRODUCES A CUPFUL OF MUCUS EVERY DAY.

FALSE

It's tricky to work out just how much mucus (snot) your nose and sinuses make, because it varies from person to person. Scientists have estimated that it can be up to a quart a day, most of which will be swallowed. Snot traps dirt, pollen and germs and stops them from getting into your lungs, which could make you very sick. The mucus near your nostrils dries out around the particles, forming a green lump, or booger. The rest of the mucus slides down your throat. Yuck!

2. YOUR EARS HELP YOU KEEP YOUR BALANCE.

TRUE

Ears aren't just for hearing. When you move around, a liquid inside part of your inner ear, or "labyrinth," moves with you, sending messages to the brain to tell it how your head is angled and whether it is rotated. It is this, along with visual information from your eyes and feedback from your muscles, that helps your brain keep you balanced.

3. DOUBLE-JOINTED PEOPLE ARE VERY BENDY BECAUSE THEY HAVE EXTRA JOINTS.

FALSE

Being double-jointed, or "hypermobile," doesn't happen because people have extra joints. It is a condition where people have loose, stretchy ligaments, which are tissues that control movement in your joints. This allows their joints to move farther. It can also happen if the person has shallow bone sockets, for example in the hips and shoulders, which means that the joints can easily pop out of place.

4. SMELLY FOODS MAKE YOU FART.

FALSE

Flatulence, or "farting," happens for several reasons, but it has nothing to do with how smelly a food is. Swallowing air can make you fart, as can eating foods that produce lots of gas as your body digests them. Some of the worst offenders are Brussels sprouts, lentils, onions, and beans. Being constipated or having a bowel problem can also cause flatulence. Ooops!

5. HEAD LICE CAN JUMP FROM ONE HUMAN HEAD TO ANOTHER.

FALSE

Head lice are wingless insects, so they can't fly. They like to live on human heads, where they feed on blood from the scalp. When people are sitting with their heads very close together, such as when they are playing, lice can crawl from one head to another. Once settled in, a female louse lays hundreds of eggs, or "nits," that hatch and start to feed. Head lice aren't dangerous, but they are very itchy!

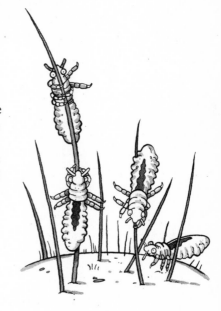

6. BAD BREATH COMES FROM NOT CLEANING YOUR TEETH.

TRUE

If you don't brush and floss daily, food particles get stuck in your mouth. The particles are gradually broken down by the bacteria that live on the teeth, tongue, and gums. This releases the same chemicals that give rotten eggs their stinky odor, and it can make your mouth smell really bad. People can also have bad breath if they have a dry mouth, eat smelly foods, such as onions and garlic, or smoke. So you know what to do—brush and floss your pearly whites and the stinky smells will stay away!

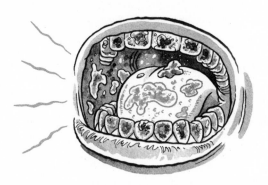

7. THERE CAN BE UP TO 10 MILLION BACTERIA ON A HUMAN HAND.

TRUE

Our bodies are covered in bacteria, but most are harmless. Your hands can have anywhere between 10,000 and 10 million bacteria on them, made up of around 150 species. Strangely, scientists have found that the species of bacteria may vary from hand to hand—so much so that the bacteria on your left hand may be very different from that on your right. As for invisible nasties, after a trip to the bathroom, the number of germs on your fingertips doubles, so don't forget to wash your hands and dry them thoroughly—wet hands spread germs more easily.

Would You Believe It?

People do some very peculiar things, but some of the following facts are so unbelievably weird that they can't possibly be true—or can they? You decide, then turn to pages 134–137 to see if you were right.

THE FACTS	TRUE	FALSE
1. The world's hottest chili pepper is 10 times hotter than tabasco sauce.	◯	◯
2. In 1957 an April Fool's joke convinced people that spaghetti grows on trees.	◯	◯
3. In Oregon, competitors race around a lake in giant pumpkins.	◯	◯
4. Octopush is an underwater hockey game.	◯	◯
5. The original name for the Google search engine was BackRub.	◯	◯
6. During World War II the government began setting fashion requirements so there was enough fabric available to make parachutes and uniforms.	◯	◯
7. Competitors in extreme ironing have to iron as much as they can in a day.	◯	◯
8. In the 18th century, birds nested in women's elaborate hairstyles.	◯	◯
9. The shortest war in history lasted just 38 minutes.	◯	◯

1. THE WORLD'S HOTTEST CHILI PEPPER IS 10 TIMES HOTTER THAN TABASCO SAUCE.

FALSE

A pepper's chili fire is measured using the Scoville Heat Unit, or SHU. The Infinity chili pepper is a whopping 235 times hotter than tabasco sauce. Tabasco sauce has a SHU of around 5,000, whereas the Infinity chili scores 1,176,182. Now that's hot!

2. IN 1957 AN APRIL FOOL'S JOKE CONVINCED PEOPLE THAT SPAGHETTI GROWS ON TREES.

TRUE

Back in 1957, spaghetti wasn't as widely eaten as it is today. On TV a spoof documentary was broadcast in the UK showing women "harvesting" spaghetti that was draped on the branches of trees. Some people watching the show were so eager to grow their own spaghetti that they called the TV station to find out where they could buy spaghetti trees!

3. IN OREGON, COMPETITORS RACE AROUND A LAKE IN GIANT PUMPKINS.

TRUE

Every October on Lake Tualatin, Oregon, the Giant Pumpkin Regatta is held. There are four races, but before they start, competitors must grab a pumpkin and hollow it out. They then sit in it and float away, paddling around a lake. Ideally, the giant pumpkins should weigh between 600 and 800 pounds (272 and 363 kg). Bigger pumpkins tend to be too slow, but 2010's winner weighed a mighty 1,200 pounds (544 kg).

4. OCTOPUSH IS AN UNDERWATER HOCKEY GAME.

TRUE

This fast and furious underwater sport takes place at the bottom of a swimming pool. Teams play with small handheld sticks that they use to push a puck into the opposing team's goal. The athletes wear a mask, fins, and snorkel, and action happens in brief spurts, between swimming to the surface for air.

5. THE ORIGINAL NAME FOR THE GOOGLE SEARCH ENGINE WAS BACKRUB.

TRUE

In 1996, founders Larry Page and Sergey Brin began the search engine but after a year decided it needed a new name. They came up with Google, playing on the word "googol," a mathematical term that represents the numeral 1 followed by 100 zeros. The use of the term reflects their mission to systemize an infinite amount of information on the Web.

6. DURING WORLD WAR II THE GOVERNMENT BEGAN SETTING FASHION REQUIREMENTS SO THERE WAS ENOUGH FABRIC AVAILABLE TO MAKE PARACHUTES AND UNIFORMS.

TRUE

In order to save materials such as wool and silk, which was used for making uniforms and parachutes, first the British and later the American governments passed bills limiting fabric usage. For example, a man's pants could not have pleats or cuffs, and the only colors they came in were black, brown, or navy. The double-breasted coat style was banned, collar widths were slimmed down, the number of pockets was limited, and skirts could not be made from more than two and a half yards of fabric.

7. COMPETITORS IN EXTREME IRONING HAVE TO IRON AS MUCH AS THEY CAN IN A DAY.

FALSE

The truth is even stranger. Extreme ironing is one of the craziest "sports" around. It started when two mountaineers set a record for ironing at the highest-ever altitude, on a Swiss mountain. Since then, people have done it while they ski, canoe, or scuba dive. The only rules are that the garment must be at least the size of a dish towel, the iron real, and the board over 3.2 feet (1 m) long.

8. IN THE 18TH CENTURY, BIRDS NESTED IN WOMEN'S ELABORATE HAIRSTYLES.

FALSE

In the 18th century it was fashionable to wear huge, elaborate wigs or hairpieces. Some rich people had these wigs built around wire frames, finished off with incredible decorations. The craze was led by Marie Antoinette, the queen of France, whose wig designs even included a model ship! The horsehair and powder that the wigs, or "poufs," were made of were ideal homes for pests such as lice and fleas, so it's likely that they made themselves right at home, even if there were no birds!

9. THE SHORTEST WAR IN HISTORY LASTED JUST 38 MINUTES.

TRUE

The Anglo-Zanzibar War took place on August 27, 1896. It began with the death of the Sultan of Zanzibar and the throne being seized by Khalid bin Barghash. British forces opened fire on the palace from their ships, and just 38 minutes later Barghash surrendered.

Your Score

Keep a record of how many answers you got right in each section in the chart below. There are 200 in all. Then add up your scores to determine your grand total.

CHAPTER	HOW MANY DID YOU SCORE?
BIZARRE BEASTIES	
TERRIBLE TEETH	
EAT OR BE EATEN	
SERIOUS SURVIVAL SKILLS	
SUPERPOWERS	
PECULIAR PARENTING	
DELIGHTFUL DINOS	
HORRIBLE HABITS	
HIGHEST, HOTTEST, DEEPEST, FASTEST	
DANGER! DANGER!	
WACKY WEATHER	
HARD ROCKS	

OMINOUS OCEANS	
LETHAL LANDSCAPES	
FANTASTIC FORMATIONS	
TERRIFIC TECHNOLOGY	
DRAMATIC DISCOVERIES	
BONKERS BIOLOGY	
OUT OF THIS WORLD	
WEIRD SCIENCE	
CURIOUS CURES	
INGENIOUS INVENTIONS	
AMAZING ANCIENTS	
HEROES AND HEROINES	
MAD, BAD, AND DANGEROUS TO KNOW	
EXOTIC EXPLORERS	
MAN-MADE MADNESS	
BRILLIANT BODIES	
WOULD YOU BELIEVE IT?	
GRAND TOTAL	

Index